ANOTHER SECOND CHANCE

THE POWER OF GRACE

KATHRYN JOHNSON

All Scripture quotations are taken from the following resources:

Scriptures using the reference KJV are from The Official King James Bible – Authorized Version (KJV)
Scripture referencing NIV are from:http://www.biblestudytools.com/niv/
Scriptures referencing AMP are from: The Amplified Bible present on Bible Gateway matches the 1987 printing:
ttps://www.biblegateway.com/versions/Amplified-Bible-AMP/

ISBN 13: 978-1517456900

ISBN 10: 1517456908

ACKNOWLEDGEMENTS

I thank God first and foremost for continuing to be with me on this incredible journey through this life and into eternity. I also want to thank my husband Eric Johnson who has taught me more about patience and unconditional love than anyone I have ever met. I thank my children, Desirae and Bryant Washington for continuing to be the inspiration for my prayers and my spiritual growth and the greatest source of my joy. I thank my dad, Richard Keyes for providing a perfect example of selfless service and love and for abounding in wisdom and grace. I would also like to thank Pastor's Edward and Patricia Thomas for always being faithful to the obedience of Christ and living lives that are a true reflection of the love of God. Lastly, I want to thank Rowena Mondares, and Leane Lima who gave of their time and talents and always encouraged me to believe that this book would one day be a tool in the hand of God that would help others.

CONTENTS

INTRODUCTION:

It is difficult to imagine that you are in the middle of a breakthrough at the very moment in your life when you feel your situation is the most unbearable.   In fact, though God is not the source of it, He often does some of His best work in us in the midst of our pain.   I realize the thought of something good coming out of something that feels so bad might be a hard concept to grasp.   We need only consider the method used to bring forth any great harvest to understand God's process for generating the best fruit in each of us.

Each year, I go through the tedious process of pruning my precious rose bushes.   As arduous as this task can be, cutting away the wilted roses from the bush is necessary if I want to assure that it produces beautiful fragrant blooms. When the blooms emerge, they are so big and fragrant. Not only do I get to enjoy them, but anyone who passes by my house can see and smell them.

In horticulture, you learn that pruning is the selective removal of parts of a plant to improve or maintain its life.   The result of pruning causes a chain reaction inside the plant and over time, the effects can clearly be seen on the outside.   If you looked at the

1

evidence of a freshly pruned plant, it might appear to the casual onlooker like a brutal process. You might see several limbs, branches, or dead blooms lying near the plant and it is difficult to imagine that a new stronger plant will emerge from what's left.

This is where my journey truly began. Like my roses, my life was in the midst of being pruned. God was answering a lifetime of my prayers to reach a place of understanding and intimacy I had yet to fully experience in Him, but first a cutting away of old things was needed.

How, you may ask, do you pick up the pieces when everything that was your sense of place and purpose is gone; all the familiar "trappings" are no longer there to lean on and you find yourself lost? You hear people say that it will get better, that you will get through this, but how? Pain can sometimes feel like a prison. To think a place that feels rooted in so much pain could actually be a beginning is sometimes unimaginable. Being stripped of your idea of safe refuge is often the first step to reaching for God's true security and the real you. The identity that you've developed around the things that make up your everyday life is sometimes a false one. Part of God's great plan of reconciling us to Himself was that we receive abundant life. There are times when this requires letting go of the life we currently have; dying to the

2

things you have learned, come to expect, or have become accustomed to.

I can only tell you that the fact that I am writing this book at all is a testament to the reality that there is life after death! I am not referring to the physical death that we will all surely face one day, unless the rapture comes first. I am referring to the death of our flesh.

There is that part of man that lives bound by the rules of life's experiences and his six senses. Though what we experience seems very real, it may not always be true. The Spirit of Truth; the Holy Spirit, is able to dispel the old way of thinking that could be keeping us bound to our fears and doubts. He does this by introducing new ideas that are in line with God. The old must die so that the new can live! This process, like the pruning of our precious plants, may look disparaging. Still from it, an abundance of spiritual fruit can spring forth that becomes the evidence to a lost world. This testimony is a proclamation of Gods creative power at work through our faith.

In the midst of our impossible places, we often find that our ears are keenly attuned to Gods voice. It is here in His presence that we can find the strength to admit we need His guidance and wisdom. We can choose to change our minds. New behaviors that lead to a new life begin with a new way of thinking about some of the same situations. Our delusions of what is normal or acceptable can keep us far too long in bondage to a life that will never lead us to the peaceful abundant life God promised. The good news is that once we allow Christ to lead, He will give you another chance. It is no consequence to God that you may have already had several *second chances*. Even if you've tried and failed countless times before, don't give up hope. I would like to share with you some of my life's experiences in the hope that my simple stories will lead you into the arms of the God of, ***Another Second Chance.***

This book contains a portion of my testimony and provides a glimpse at how greatly one's beliefs ultimately control the quality of their life. In it, I share the influence the Ten Commandments and in fact many of the laws contained in the Old Testament of the Bible had on my life. These laws required that I earn my rewards from God. Those rewards, good or bad, were a direct result of how well I justified myself through my own efforts. Unable to do this apart from God, I feel into hopelessness and even though I was actively ministering to others, I was unable, ultimately, to rescue myself. Each chapter unveils how beautifully God

4

revealed Himself to me and orchestrated my total surrender to His perfect will for my life. The book allows you to become a witness to the power of God's grace in my life as I move from hopelessness to empowerment.

CHAPTER 1

WHO'S IN CONTROL?

At 41 years old, I felt I had weathered enough storms with God to know how to survive the season I was about to enter. I knew after struggling with my marriage for almost 20 years and wrestling with a small flailing church for half that time, that it was time for some life changing decisions.

My husband and I had shared a house for almost twenty years, but it had been a long time since we shared a life together. We met when we were both young; I was only 18 at the time and he was 19. We dated for almost five years before marrying so I knew very well that we lived two very different lifestyles. He was a socialite who loved to be out and about socializing with friends. I was a lot more conservative and kind of awkward in social settings. Having joined a church when I was 16, I didn't ever really do the party scene till I met him.

Nine months after we married I gave birth to my daughter and two years later we had our son. Though from the beginning we wrestled over our ideas of what was appropriate in our relationship, at first, we still managed to have a lot of youthful fun. Our two small children kept us busy, and the dreams we shared about a better future together gave me hope that the daily sorrows would one day end and it would all somehow be better.

Many folks thought we were too young to get married and too immature. Looking back, I know this was probably true, but you couldn't tell me that then. I firmly believed that even though we had fought over the years about the differences in our personalities and just about everything else, and even though we did not both feel the same about God, love and marriage would conquer it all. He wasn't done partying and I was still a childlike dreamer. I was convinced that the fantasies I envisioned about my life would somehow magically come true if only I could hang in there and weather our storms. We shared some beautiful times with our children and more holidays and family occasions than I can remember. Unfortunately, what we never shared was an intimate relationship. It is so important to be really good

8

friends and I'm not sure we ever were. I absolutely loved him, but there were a lot of things he and I both did that kept our relationship in a state of turmoil. For years I cried about it and eventually, when I realized my childlike dreams might not come true, I became bitter and distant. It wasn't just our pronounced differences on how our lives should be lived that caused conflicts for us, it was also all of the baggage we brought into our relationships from past hurts. I dealt with the fear of rejection and I needed him to be my knight in shining armor and I think when I realized he was just a man and one that I wasn't totally compatible with, it was devastating for me. I tried to use my faith that our relationship would change, but it was futile after twenty years of us living separately while together. I believe at different times, and in our own ways, we both tried, but I was convinced that it would take God to fix what had been broken from the very beginning. Our relationship had not been built on a foundation in God nor was it rooted in God when we parted. I believe, in fact, that after so many years of throwing God and my work in the church at him, he didn't see God and especially not the church as a viable solution for our problems.

He was busy with his construction business and his friends and I buried myself in church and family hoping that if I had enough faith, God could fix everything. I wanted things to be different and I longed for an intimate relationship with him, but I had absolutely no idea how to bridge the gap between us. By the end of our marriage, even when we did try to spend time together, it was forced and tense. Over the years because we weren't really sharing our lives, we became like two roommates. It wasn't hostile, we were just distant. We came together on occasion for family vacations or gatherings, but for the most part, we lived two separate lives.

I know that some may wonder how we stayed together for so long; we just went about living our lives and the years rolled by. I wish I had a more profound answer and it may seem oversimplified, but basically, we shifted into doing things day after day and life went on. I didn't say it was always happy or fulfilling, but it went on. You get busy with stuff; working and potty training, transporting kids to different places, church activities, holidays, and doing all the things you're doing and the years pass. Even unhappiness and loneliness can become a way of life. It shouldn't be, but for so many people, it is. Some of them self-medicate to get through it, using things like alcohol or drugs. My medicine was a fanatical search for God's approval.

Looking back, it's crazy just how quickly the years passed. Of course when I was living through those years they seemed to be never-ending. I remember feeling very lonely and hopeless sometimes and I wondered why no one appeared to notice. I wanted to hide how I felt from the world while at the same time I wanted someone to see how desperate I felt and help me. I really wanted my husband to help me, but neither of us was capable of helping ourselves, much less each other. We were two broken people who fell into lust and then conditional love and marriage, but that wasn't enough to sustain a lifelong relationship.

While there were times when we supported each other's interests, we just never really found our way into a trusting friendship and relationship. A healthy relationship requires a commitment to spend quality time with someone continuing to invest in who they are and are becoming.

 As the distance between our daily routines became more pronounced, I spent more and more time working for the church and he spent more and more time building his business and doing things he enjoyed. We each had a picture of the life we desired to live. The problem was over the years; the pictures changed and were no longer the same. We lived in two different worlds colliding on occasion, primarily for the sake of our children, but by the end of our marriage, we weren't even fighting anymore. For me, it had just become an anguished silence. The hope that I once had of transforming our marriage and sharing a life with my husband was gone, replaced with an overwhelming sense of sadness.

As I prepared to leave that night, my mind raced and I wasn't even sure of where I was going, just away from where I was. After years of laboring with this decision, suddenly, my mind made up, I had to leave. I cannot begin to describe the guilt I felt at leaving. Have I failed as a Christian, I wondered. "Why isn't my faith enough?" My failure in marriage was to me, a failure in God. This was such a hard thing for my already troubled self-esteem to deal with. How could a minister of God's word fail so miserably?

I had served as an assistant to my pastor for several years and so I spent a considerable amount of time studying the Bible. I even preached, taught classes, counseled others, and had developed a large and growing women's Bible study outside of the church to empower women to trust God. Still I was unaware of the fact that I had not completely allowed God to be the head of my life. If you had asked me, I would have said God had total control, but

12

the truth was there were areas I had not trusted Him enough to let go of.

It's sometimes hard to imagine that we have the power to break through what is holding us in bondage. Women who feel victimized might say they are not in control, but often, even being a victim is a result of our choices; especially if we choose to do nothing and stay in a bad situation. I wanted the faith to change my circumstances, but wanting faith and having it are two different things. Ultimately, God has given each of us the power by faith to change our world. It all comes down to what we believe to be true. In truth, I believed the obstacles in my marriage were too big for anyone to fix, even God, and I felt powerless to change them on my own and had grown tired of trying.

It Begins with a Thought

Christ's sacrifice gave us the power of grace. *The secret to unlocking this power is to trust God so completely that we give up our right to control anything.* It is the easiest thing to say, but when you've practiced being in control, even prided yourself on being the master of your own fate for many years, it's not always easy to do. Even when it becomes clear that we need to die to our way of doing things, we still want to control the dying process. Though we pray for a change, often we fail to realize that change is wrapped up in first deciding to do things differently. You have to be willing to put to death old thought processes. These thoughts may be all you know, but they clearly have not been enough to keep you from the desperate circumstances you've found yourselves in.

The funny thing about our ideas is that if we have entertained them long enough, they become rooted in our belief system. Even when we recognize they may be obsolete, there are times when we fight adamantly to keep them. This is important for us to understand because our beliefs become the framework for our lives.

My step-mom passed away several years ago. Still, she left an indelible mark on me. She was a proud woman with fine tastes and she believed that things should be done just so. Though I was one of seven kids, my step-mom and dad did an amazing job of introducing us to new experiences. They were committed to preparing us to thrive in any environment. My sisters and I would sometimes be whisked away for weekends in Northern California or taken out to lunch at nice restaurants. Our blended family consisted of three boys and four girls and it wasn't easy or inexpensive to share these opportunities with us, yet they did. I remember during one of our outings we went to lunch at a nice restaurant. I was eating a bowl of clam chowder when without thinking; I scooped the food up moving my spoon toward me, banging the spoon on the bottom and sides of the bowl as I did. My mom quickly took the time to correct me, "Always push the spoon away from you and don't touch the bowl with the spoon. You shouldn't make noises like that while eating and you don't want to push your food into your lap." I was about 14 at the time, not impressed at all with her wisdom, and frankly annoyed that as hungry as I was, I couldn't just eat my soup. She continued over the years, as the opportunity presented itself, to remind me of this *rule* and eventually, I believed this idea to be correct. I thought that this was in fact not just a way, but the right way to eat from a bowl when in public. Now it may seem like a small thing, but though I never said anything to anyone else, I was conscious of others as they banged their spoon noisily on the side of their bowl or spooned their soup toward themselves. It wasn't a point of contention for me, but I definitely felt the way I had been taught was the best way.

This seems like the most insignificant issue, and yet it is an example of one of hundreds, thousands of ideas that become the vantage point from which we see our world and those we share it with. If we truly want to rise from the ashes of our pain, we have to be willing to accept that some of the framework we've built our lives on might be faulty. We may need to dramatically change the way we see things in order to receive what we are asking from God. I was crying out for peace, but had conformed to the ideas of those around me. While this isn't always wrong, if we want a life that is consistent with God's plan, *the truths we believe must always line up with God's word, or we will have to renew our minds.*

Romans 12:2 (KJV) [2]And be not conformed to this world: but be ye transformed by the renewing of your mind, that ye may prove what is that good, and acceptable, and perfect, will of God.

It wasn't until I had kids and didn't have time to eat, much less think of how many times my spoon hit the bottom of a bowl that I realized this might not have had quite the importance I gave it. Don't get me wrong, my lessons in manners have served me well and I would dare say I could eat with British royalty, but a different way of thinking presented itself and it challenged my old ideas and ultimately replaced them. My mind was transformed by the information I received and a better renewed mind emerged.

Often we fight to maintain our ideas of what is right. I believe we fight even harder about what we believe to be Godly. I was amazed at how much of what I believed to be true, even about God, was refined in the midst of my pain. It's not that God hadn't tried to gently speak to me, but there is something about the fire of affliction that has a way of getting our full attention. It can burn off the baggage we've packed around our lives and for some, carried many years. Sometimes, we've wrapped several layers of our traditions and ideas around God's actual intent and if we are truly to receive His best, we have to allow the layers to come off. We have to give up control.

If you had asked me, I would have argued that my life was in accordance with the roadmap God had designed for me, but I was about to discover that this was only true in some areas; those that I had been willing to relinquish to His loving care. There were places in my life that my flesh was still ruling me. This is a problem. We can't be ruled by two masters.

Matthew 6:24 (KJV) No man can serve two masters: for either he will hate the one, and love the other; or else he will hold to the one, and despise the other. Ye cannot serve God and mammon.

This was exactly what I was guilty of, though at the time I didn't know it. I was serving God, but also trying to control my own circumstances.

Erecting Walls

I believe that when we reach what we perceive to be our lowest point, we either give up, or begin to take serious stock in where we are and how we got there. I muddled along for years, dealing with depression and low self-esteem, but never stopped long enough to make an assessment of my life toward really changing it. It is like having a chronic nagging headache and taking a different medication each day. You may find something that provides temporary relief, but the pain never fully goes away. Unresolved issues can stack up for months, even years without our ever being fully aware of them. Instead of dealing with my fears and pain, some of them, I pressed down and covered up with a wall that I had constructed over several years. I looked up one day and discovered I was God's child, but also an angry, bitter, and even at times, vindictive person. This truth, more than my frustration, hurt, pain, or anger was the catalyst for finally recognizing my need for changes. Among them was ending my twenty year marriage. I once saw a sign that read "If you don't like what you see, don't blame the mirror, change the image." I was a minister of love, who was so engrossed in the steps that demonstrate the love of God; but I wasn't actually experiencing it.

Long before I met my husband at age 19, I had already developed some pretty strong ideas about my self-worth, or should I say lack of it. My parents divorced when I was around nine and like so many kids, I felt somehow personally responsible for their split. It was as if they not only rejected each other, but me too. A few years after the divorce, my siblings and I left the home we shared with our mom in Ohio to live with our dad in California. It was a new place filled with new possibilities, but also a strange place where I no longer had the comfort of my cousins and other extended family members. I was lonely for them and my mom, but not prepared to leave my dad and new family. This was a constant dilemma for me and though I considered leaving for years, I couldn't even bear the thought of being away from my father. I tried to hide my true feelings and instead began acting out with my stepmom. I admired her, and recognized immediately that my life was better because of her, but I also perceived her to be part of the reason for my constant inner turmoil. It doesn't make sense, but I thought, if not for her, my parents could somehow have reconciled their differences. At the same time, however, I loved her dearly and didn't want to imagine my life without her either. She was a counselor at the elementary school that I attended the first fall after we moved to California. Many of the students quickly discovered that I was her daughter and immediately took a disliking to me. I was lonely for home and my old life and didn't assimilate well to the new environment. Often, I could be found sitting on a curb with a book or alone somewhere. My silent pain was interpreted as being stuck up and a group of girls began to bully me. They eventually went from just harsh words to pushing and hitting me. This went on for a while until my teacher finally walked into a classroom where they had me cornered one day and witnessed their abuse. They were promptly dealt with, but not before I added a few more bricks to the wall of resentment, fear, and pain I was erecting. This was the beginning of a pattern of teasing and bullying that went on through Jr. High school. Thanks to my long skinny legs and feet, I was a perfect target for teasing. I secretly wanted to be popular, but instead felt awkward and ugly. The wall around my heart continued to be erected too, though likely not noticeable to those around me because I was such a practical joker. I was known for making everyone laugh, but often, deep inside, I was crying.

By the age of 16 I was already struggling with thoughts of suicide. I believe that when you are convinced that your life is meaningless, and each day seems more hopeless and futile than the day before, death seems like an opportunity to finally rest. Of course this is far from the truth since our spirits will live on forever somewhere. Still, at the time, it felt like a good option. Instead, God, in His mercy, introduced another option.

I had never been a regular church goer, but thought it might give me the solace I needed so I became a member of a small church my grandmother attended and often invited us to. I was, for the most part, just a member of an organization. The church was primarily older people, or so it seemed to me at the time. Still I was drawn to it and just the act of attending church made me feel somewhat better - more worthy, so I continued to go off and on for years, still battling with a strong desire to end my life.

Though never fully reconciling my value in God, one thing that did manifest from my years of attending various churches was the desire to serve others. By the time I met my husband, I was entrenched in the idea that my self-worth was somehow strangely dependent on my ability to help other people. By then I had several years during which a wall of mistrust, shame, pain, and a host of other emotions was deeply rooted. I knew as I began a five-year courtship and later marriage to my ex-husband that we were very different from each other. He was a very social person; I was awkward in most social settings except those that included my family and later my church family. He was a risk taker who loved spontaneity and I preferred to have a plan for almost everything. Even with our differences, I was convinced that our love and my ability to *help* him would be enough to keep us together. Love can go a long way, even when it is not perfect love. Having two kids, a mortgage, a thriving business, and several cars and homes were also factors that ensured that we stayed together for twenty years. Still, I married someone who I was not only very different from, but who had his own issues and expectations of what our relationship should be. Though we created some incredible children and memories, there were also a lot of disappointments and tears.

After many years of trying to "fix" my husband, I realized that it is difficult if not impossible to help someone along their journey if you don't even know where you are headed. My life was full, but not fulfilled and I fought off and on with depression. I was raising two beautiful kids, had returned to school and was working my way up the ladder on my job. Still, I didn't feel good about my life.

My busy life also included a number of activities in the church. I worked with the small congregation I was a member of by then, to feed the hungry and organized food and clothing drives. I didn't realize at the time I needed those I was serving more than they needed me. For a long time, I was able to take the edge off of my feelings of low self-worth by working to make the lives of others better. When the issues you face are inside of you, however, and you refuse to truly unearth them and confront them, after a while, it doesn't even matter how much people affirm you, it won't be enough.

My work in the church became all-consuming and my husband had his own interests with different business schemes and social activities. This caused resentment between us and we frequently did things separately, even though we shared the same house. We clashed about our differing ideas; the lack of time we spent together, our kids, and finances.

This condition only intensified when I decided to return to school in addition to the other roles I was already playing. I remember vividly the day that God moved divinely to give me a push toward finishing my education. I was arguing with my husband about money. I wanted some and he was reluctant to give it to me. Shopping was one of the things I used as a distraction from my depression and a substitute for real deliverance from my pain. After our heated discussion, as I sat with my daughter who had witnessed our conversation, she turned to me and said, "I wish you had your own money." I don't know if it was her facial expression, or the tone of her voice, but that simple sentence spoke volumes to me. What was I teaching my daughter through my life? What was she learning from me? It was one of those divine moments where God used a child to speak destiny into me. I went away and cried silently. There was something about looking into the face of my daughter that day and seeing what I felt was her disappointment with my life that gave me a new dedication to change. I have often heard that God moves in mysterious ways, well that day, He moved through the voice of a child. I had been wrestling with the idea of finishing my degree and that conversation was the final push I needed to go back to school. I was convinced that greater education would equate to greater opportunities. It wasn't an easy decision. I was already juggling a family and full-time job in addition to the church. I was determined, however to provide a different example for her and "get my own money." This is in fact exactly what I did. I worked for the next four years and earned not only a bachelor's degree, but a master's. This education along with the years of experience I had on my job allowed me to move from a receptionist to upper management. This was nothing short of a miracle, but over time, I "got my own money." I gained more than the money, however. God used my daughter and my dissatisfaction to move me from a place of complacency to a place of accomplishment. What a boost to my self-confidence that was. I began to organize even larger community outreach events and was even acknowledged with awards for my community service by local government and my peers at the university where I worked. I felt honored, but not fulfilled. God was indeed doing miracles through me, but I had yet to yield myself fully to Him.

Sadly, the same miracles did not take place in my marriage. The time I spent on my education and on climbing the corporate ladder only drove my husband and I further apart. By the end of our marriage, we were like two roommates sharing the same house but not the same life. I was angry that he had not magically transformed into the husband I dreamed he should be after all my years of trying to "fix" him and I'm sure he was disappointed with me too. My disappointment turned to bitterness. I had built up a wall of resentment toward him and felt absolutely justified in burying myself in other interests and causes instead of trying to invest in our marriage. I was tired from all the years I felt I had already tried and now, I just wanted God to somehow, fix it, fix him! Part of the problem was that I was not a witness for God's goodness, but instead a wounded vessel that was capable of wounding others. There is no room for bitterness in a vessel of honor that was fashioned in the image of Christ. All the accomplishments and accolades in the world don't replace being acceptable and pleasing to God.

I hid from my pain and regrettably the wall I had erected over many years kept the pain in rather than expose me to the healing power of Jesus. Instead of shielding me from years of toxic feelings, the wall had actually locked them in and kept me from fully receiving the love of God. Behind that wall and buried beneath my true fears were the best parts of me. In place of building lives on a foundation of God's truths, we often erect walls of resentment around the lies we have believed for many years, even lies we have told ourselves. Over and over again in my mind, I played a sad testimony to myself that helped to keep me bound to despair. 'You're useless, unlovable, that's why you're a victim, and bad things happen to you." Erecting walls of any kind is unacceptable. They can be built by those of us with good intentions who simply feel we need to be protected. All of the protection we will ever need can be found in the arms of our God.

At this point, I had no idea how to fully trust in God or understand who He wanted to be in my life, so I fought my own battles and hid behind the wall I had been building for years. I hid so long behind those walls, when the pain that was my life finally forced me to emerge, I truly didn't even know who I was. I was terrified and shocked that I couldn't even define what my life needed to look like to ensure that it lined up with the abundant life in Christ I had been promised. What I was sure of was that I wasn't fully living that life.

Receive Him

As God's creations, we are fashioned to hold His Spirit. To realize our truest selves, we have to be open to receiving Christ. The walls were my way of regulating who had access to me, but unbeknownst to me, that included God. I tried desperately, for years, to self-medicate using a "prescription" of toxic things in the world. This included codependent relationships, creating unnecessary debt, even prescribed medicine for the various illnesses that developed out of my stress and pain. So many times our quest to be filled leaves us disappointed and subsequently angry with those we share our lives with. You can never fill the void that God fashioned to contain His Spirit with a substitute god. When we do this, it is easier than you might imagine to create unrealistic expectations of how those we share our lives with should fill that void. I tried to put my husband, children, and those around me in the place that only God should be and that did not work. I thought I was giving perfect love, but that is impossible to do if you are not receiving it. The walls had to go, but first I needed a new way of thinking.

The problem was that I was afraid of being wrong about what I had believed all those years concerning God. For many years, though challenged from time to time, I brushed off any suggestion that my way of thinking was wrong and assumed those who challenged my facts were ignorant. In doing this, I was able to hang onto what I believed was true.

Isaiah 55:8-9 (KJV) For my thoughts *are* not your thoughts, neither *are* your ways my ways, saith the LORD. ⁹ For *as* the heavens are higher than the earth, so are my ways higher than your ways, and my thoughts than your thoughts.

The idea of giving up control of my life was an even bigger challenge for me because I felt I had so little control of it. The few things I did control, I didn't want to relinquish. I clung to God as my personal source of strength, hope and comfort. To even imagine that the ideas I had formed around God were wrong ideas was something that would make me defensive, even hostile!

It wasn't that I had learned nothing in the many years of sitting in church. The fact that I was still living and serving was a testament to the truths I had received. Total liberty, however, is the result of allowing God to reveal heavenly truths that are higher than our facts and are often buried under the layers of our experiences, traditions, thoughts and ideas. I was empowered to a degree, but still more bound to wrong ideas than I knew. If we are not careful, we can get stuck in the mode of doing what appears to be all the right things, in the right places for all the wrong reasons. For example, I was strengthened by the fact that God would be my help in time of trouble. I was also comforted by the fact that He was a just God. This justice, I believed would be the way in which I would get my fair share if I was only good enough. I held on to the idea that He was just and fair and rewarded our good works and punished our failures. If I did a good job I could expect something good in return; this I could relate to. I wasn't afraid to work hard, I had been doing that most of my life; working to gain approval and love. The problem with believing this way is that even when trials come to test your faith, you interpret them to mean you've lost value in the eyes of God. I often thought that if I was facing a trial, it must be the result of doing something wrong. Every challenging situation became a personal failure. This is what I struggled with. Any failure or frailty on my part was confirmation to me of my inability to be loved. I couldn't even please God who I was taught loved everyone! Out of this place of constant feelings of unworthiness, I served others. My desire to share God with others wasn't wrong, it was my desperate need to justify my worth in doing the things I did for God that was wrong. Now and then I would hear the Spirit of God say, "Who was that for, or that was for you, to make you feel better." It was something that angered me each time I heard it. All my hard work and efforts to help others; I was insulted at the thought that it wasn't exclusively for their benefit and God's glory. Don't get me wrong, I loved people and had a true heart to serve them, but I was also trying to obtain God's favor and His reward of a better life. I was taught that good people do good things and I didn't know that these good things must come out of a heart that is good; I believed the manifestation on the outside was the primary indicator of what was going on on the inside. Right or wrong, I felt my beliefs had sustained me to that point, and I was not willing to even consider ideas that suggested I would have to abandon them.

There is a vast difference between the way we think and the way God thinks. God is the perfect father and He wants what's best for us. There are times when we want our way at any cost even if it's not what God desires for us. Galatians 5:17 points out that the *flesh yearns for what is contrary to the Spirit.* If what we want is the very opposite of what is best for us, God is never, never going to provide it. We may, through our persistence, obtain it, but it's not from God and He won't bless our efforts or fix the outcome of our works until we turn them over to Him. Man is prone to judging people and circumstances based on our senses. We are quick to draw conclusions and even act based on what we have or are experiencing. If we see it, feel it, taste it, hear it, touch it, or smell it we think we can believe it's true and put our trust in it. Our thoughts and beliefs simply can't be trusted! God's provision requires God's thinking. We must do things His way.

I was in a broken state, because I yielded more to my way than God's way. I was working so hard on His behalf that I no longer recognized His will. This is how I ended up, after many years of marriage, realizing that I had come to the end of it. Still, I was so uncertain about the next phase of my life, I was afraid to take the next step.

Starting Over

It is possible to be fully aware that the next step requires you to separate yourself from almost everything you've been, but be so paralyzed by fear, you linger long after Gods provision has left your circumstance. Fear of the unknown can strap you into an emotional rollercoaster that seems never-ending. One day you're up the next your down; your emotions completely governed by the circumstances surrounding you. If my relationship, or job, or other situations were going well, I was alright, if they weren't, I was struggling. Even though I had perfected the ability to hide those struggles from most of the world, the years of challenges were beginning to wear on me. I noticed the longer I remained in these situations, the more exposed my real feelings became to those closest to me. Though I chose to shut my eyes to the image I had become, there was ultimately no mistaking my reflection in the eyes of others. I remember once my little sister asking me, "Are you happy?" I answered in my most humble long suffering servant's voice I could muster, "The joy of the Lord is my strength." She looked at me with a mixture of annoyance and sorrow and asked the question again. I reassured her I was fine, but later pondered the question myself. It is great to have people around you that accept you unconditionally, but even better to have those around you that see you through the eyes of God and press you to be nothing less than what He has created you to be.

Sometimes we need someone who will not accept our contradictory lives.

We often align ourselves with people who make us feel good; it is so much wiser to share our lives with folks who will help us to be all that God desires. When I was a kid, my best friend and I went to both junior high and high school together. We had been friends for years, but when we got to high school, she wanted to be a part of a more popular group of kids. I shared my concerns, but she enjoyed the life they offered and their influence became more important than mine. We eventually grew apart, I was in the church by then and she began to do things that were *fun*. I remember her referring to me in front of her friends one time as a "square." I felt so ashamed and hurt. We were both kids with issues, but I had turned to the church and she had turned to a group of friends that made her feel better, but they were not good for her. Years later, after high school, we connected again. By then she had had a baby and at one point was kicked out of her parents' home. I let her stay with me for a bit. She went on to get married and have more kids and did just fine, but her early years are a vivid reminder of what can happen when we satisfy our desire to feel good above God's desire that we have what is best for us.

It took my broken state for me to fully recognize that the word of God was only a compass if I followed it. You can't follow it halfway and then go down your own path. I would never reach the destinations I dreamed of if I continued to follow the same old paths; doing the same things day after day and somehow miraculously expecting a different outcome. The challenge was in finding the courage to put an end to the things that were clearly leading me in a direction that God was not going in. My focus was no longer on fixing my husband, or my job, or even my children. First, I had to fix me.

I would never encourage anyone to leave a marriage without giving it everything you've got and standing in faith that God can and will restore it. He is, after all, the God of reconciliation, but I had lost both the hope that my marriage could be restored and even worse that my life could be renewed. I finally made one of the most painful decisions I've ever had to make; I packed my clothes in a few garbage bags and left my home. Not long after, I found myself in a small apartment in the dark. Night after night I went through an almost surreal ritual; waking up on the floor and sitting straight up wondering where I was.

From the bed of the house I had shared with my soon-to-be ex-husband and children, I could see moonlight through the French doors that were in the sunroom just off our bedroom. This strange place was not my home! There was no light coming through any windows in this quiet, dark, foreign place. Each night, for many nights, I was startled as I awoke asking myself, "where am I?" It is possible to feel like you're dying and still be fully alive. I had no idea how I would make it through the night, much less the rest of my life. One thing was for sure, in the darkness, all by myself, I cried out to God like never before. "Lord speak to me! Save me!"

Mark 8:34-35 (KJV) [34] **And when he had called the people *unto him* with his disciples also, he said unto them, Whosoever will come after me, let him deny himself, and take up his cross, and follow me.**[35] **For whosoever will save his life shall lose it; but whosoever shall lose his life for my sake and the gospel's, the same shall save it.**

I have heard people speak of heart break, but never, until that moment had I truly physically felt like my heart was broken. My chest literally hurt and I was unable to find a way to stop the aching I had for what I had known. I longed for the very thing that would surely, if I had remained in it, have been the death of me. It was time to deny; to refuse to know my life as I had known it.

Though it was my decision to finally end my marriage after many years of struggling, still, I felt disappointed, alone, and utterly heartbroken. My flesh, including my ideas of how things should be done, was finally dying.

This was not the only source of my brokenness. I had also decided, along with the pastor to dissolve the church I co-pastored for several years. This was another painful decision, but necessary as I could no long handle the tremendous amount of work that was required in my broken state. It just became too much for either of us to bear. Eventually, we decided to close the church. I was in the greatest test of my faith and when most Christians turn to their church family for support, I now had no church family. So there I was facing divorce without a church home, both of which not only affected me, but tore my children's lives apart. Their sorrow became yet another cause for my pain.

I began questioning everything about my life. I couldn't turn to my friends or family because I was too embarrassed. There was just too much shame and disappointment to turn to anyone and the fact that I was still being called on to minister to others kept me putting on the face of strength while inside I was dying. How did I get here? How could I be the source of strength and direction for so many others and yet my life was so out of control?

There was no way I could have known I was in a perfect position to finally let go and listen to God. I was ready to hear truth, even if it was different from what I had clung to for the past 41 years. Though it was a painful journey, I had reached a place of empowerment and God was about to do the impossible. Finally, I surrendered.

CHAPTER 2

OK, I'M LISTENING

It would be great if I could testify that I have always been faithful in my pursuit of God and His truths. I would love to reveal that I have regularly spent long meditative hours in prayer and study. The reality of my life, up to the point of my divorce, was that this simply wasn't true. Sometimes I did and sometimes I didn't. I was a mom, a minister, a student working on a Master's Degree, a full-time employee, a daughter, a wife, a community volunteer...you get the idea. Even though I was capable of digging out nuggets to teach the word of God to others, it wasn't the same as diving in with a heart to hear what God was saying to me. I think deep down, I was afraid of what He would say. I justified my failure to listen by telling myself that I must surely be an anointed, appointed servant because people continued to show up and listen intently to what I had to say when I taught or when I preached. The more desperate my condition became, the more I abandoned my love relationship with God. It's amazing how long a *seasoned* child of God can operate on autopilot. We know just where to sing, shout, and quote the scriptures that we've committed to memory. We can be present at every church event and appear to be fully engaged in every moment, and inside, be slowly slipping away from the source of our hope and joy. I confess, looking back, this was me. Frankly, I was just plain tired.

My fatigue was partly due to the incredible amount of work I put in, but that wasn't the only reason for my weariness. I had convinced myself that all my efforts would somehow equate to a demonstration of faithfulness to God. Surely, I thought, He would see my many successes and my dedicated service and give me my heart's desire. I was tired from a mind that endlessly searched for ways to feel more worthwhile and worthy.

With all my self-efforts, still, my 20 year marriage was failing, though I tried everything I could imagine to fix it. I was confused. I thought, if this isn't enough, what does it take to receive the abundant life that God's word declares is mine? I wondered how

I would get to the place of joy and peace that so many folks around me appeared to have already arrived at. I felt I was working as hard as I could. Nonetheless, I suffered from deep rooted self-esteem issues and constantly questioned my self-worth. Worse, I questioned God's opinion of my worth, so I continued to work harder and harder growing more and more frustrated as I did. Somehow, all of that work, though tiring, made me feel more in control and with so little control over the rest of my life; this became a way to cope.

I had an identity crisis. I believe my identity crisis came from not having a clear enough picture of who Christ was in me. I knew I was called to be a reflection of Christ, but when I looked in the mirror, sometimes I just saw me.

At times I was leaning on God's unchanging hand, standing on my faith and patiently waiting on God to produce my miracle. There were some things I could wait patiently for, no matter the situation. I loved the word of God and understood it had the power to transform my mind. I held to certain truths quoting favorite scriptures every day. Scriptures like Philippians 4:19, 1 John 4:4, and Deuteronomy 28:13 were among my favorites.

Phil 4:19 (KJV) But my God shall supply all your need according to his riches in glory by Christ Jesus.

1 John (KJV) 4:4 Ye are of God, little children, and have overcome them: because greater is he that is in you, than he that is in the world.

Deuteronomy 28:13 (KJV) And the LORD shall make thee the head, and not the tail; and thou shalt be above only, and thou shalt not be beneath; if that thou hearken unto the commandments of the LORD thy God, which I command thee this day, to observe and to do *them*:

Through the power of God's word, He had already shown me the evidence of His blessings in my life, but I didn't always wait on God's answer. Sometimes, even when He provided an answer, I perceived it through my pain instead of through the Holy Spirit. It was when I began to allow what I was enduring to become bigger than God's promises that I felt He was late in answering my prayers. Many times all I was really praying for was peace in the midst of my storm. In those seasons I began to look at my simple insignificant image in the mirror and to put in the most work. I just knew that the unbearable waiting could end and my prayers could be answered if only I unlocked the door to blessings with my service. As my seasons continued, I began to feel that maybe I missed it somewhere. This must be punishment for a botched job or some past or present sin. I wracked my brain trying to figure out what I did wrong. Of course this is when the church lessons of my youth emerged and my sin conscious mind ran rampant.

Those early days of being taught God's word had literally saved me from certain death at my own hand. Unfortunately, they had also been the cause of a double dose of guilt and shame. Though I wasn't always aware of it, deep down I was convinced that I had to continue to work to show my faithfulness and worth. I can't tell you how many times the words of church folks rang in my head as they shared their interpretation of scriptures like those found in the second chapter of James: "faith without works is dead!" This left me feeling I wasn't truly justified unless I was doing something. I totally missed the idea that the works James was referring to were the actions that came after receiving by faith instructions from God. They were not intended to just be a list of self-imposed or man imposed tasks to make me feel justified.

No matter how effective my efforts actually were, I began to second guess everything, even my ability to hear the leading of the Holy Spirit. My self-doubt and feelings of worthlessness increased as my confidence in God's solution decreased. It wasn't that I didn't believe He was capable. Sometimes I asked myself would He do it for me. At other times I just didn't feel like I could wait any longer for Him to show up with an answer. In my desperation I can remember asking Him what I had done wrong. I would point out all of the accolades that others were giving me and remind God how faithful I was to His work and supporting the church. I would put Him in remembrance of His word, but often, didn't fully believe I would receive His promises. I wanted to know what else I needed to do to gain His favor. I was a good person! If my situation was dire enough, I would even begin to try and make deals with God. I think about this and smile now as I imagine the *creator of heaven and earth and all things therein* listening as I tried to convince Him of what I could do as a favor to Him if only He would do what I wanted when I wanted it.

I had faith, but it was often diminished by the blending of all of the things I had heard and believed over the years. I had mixed the messages I heard about obedience to the law and sacrifice, with the message of God's grace. I pictured God as a wonderful, loving, amazing creator, who could do great things on my behalf if only I did enough to please Him and demonstrate how holy I was.

44

Oddly enough, it was at this very low point in my life that I was teaching women that their self-esteem was rooted in allowing God alone to justify them. I taught that we should abandon the perfect images of motherhood and even womanhood that our world tried to push on us and simply look to God for our identity. What I knew was that all too often, our actions are governed by how we allow others and our circumstances to define us. We are, for example, surrounded by images of ultra-skinny women with flawless hair and skin. How can we ever measure up to what appears to be perfection? I told the women in my class that it was only when we looked to God that we could see ourselves through His eyes. I was right about allowing God to justify us. I believed if we received the idea that we were valuable to Him that no one else's opinion of us mattered. I painted a picture of our Heavenly Father peering down from His throne looking adoringly, approvingly at us no matter how many wrinkles or how much cellulite we had. I gained strength from knowing this. What I didn't fully understand at that point, is exactly what it meant to be valued by God. I also didn't understand how to obtain the favor of God and didn't know that I was working for something I already had. I spoke about simply receiving it, but I found myself working to try and obtain it. I can't tell you how many times I quoted Romans 8:29-30 to encourage both the women I was teaching and myself.

Romans 8:29-30 (KJV) [29] **For whom he did foreknow, he also did predestinate** *to be* **conformed to the image of his Son, that he might be the firstborn among many brethren.** [30] **Moreover whom he did predestinate, them he also called: and whom he called, them he also justified: and whom he justified, them he also glorified.**

What a powerful scripture this is! It declares in a few verses God's intent and takes us from before our creation through our glorification in Christ! I read this and was sure that God alone was my justifier, but I eventually discovered that that meant so much more than I had imagined. I didn't know till much later that to be justified is to be made righteous by Christ through His blood sacrifice on the cross. I also didn't fully grasp that it was perfect unconditional love that made this sacrifice possible. So much of my feelings of value were tied to the love I had received to that point. I didn't fully comprehend my worth, because I couldn't distinguish what I thought was love, based on my experiences, from the perfect love that expressed itself for me on the cross. It was as if a battle was raging between the knowledge I had amassed in my past and the truths I was now hearing. It is surprising how much of what we've endured and been taught creates a framework for how we see God.

Looking Back Moving Forward

I attended a women's retreat years ago during which a service was dedicated to clearing out any residue in our minds from our past. The speaker emphasized that often things have happened to us that we might not have a vivid memory of; things that still affected who we were in Christ. She invited us to get into a comfortable, meditative state, and to allow our thoughts to drift back in time. Each time our mind stumbled on a particularly painful memory, we were asked to remember that Jesus, the Lord of our lives was with us. She shared the sentiment of Deuteronomy 31:8, telling us that God would be with us and never, never leave us, nor would he forsake us.

It was during this exercise that I realized that I had some pain related to my childhood. God's revelation can open our eyes to truths that may have been hidden until we are able to receive them.

The lights were dimmed and soft music played. I began to hear the sound of other women crying in the room as painful memories emerged and they were forced to face them and give them to God.

47

At first I thought, I would not benefit from the exercise. Still, dutifully, I closed my eyes and began thinking about being a baby in my mother's arms. To my surprise, it wasn't long before I started having a reaction to the idea of being a baby. I suddenly had the memory of another baby taking my place. I realized in that moment that I had gone through something as a baby that though I didn't remember caused me pain and left an impression on my heart.

My mother became pregnant only a few months after I was born. My little sister was born when I was only 11 months old. She quickly became my lifelong playmate and friend. Still, she had also become my replacement. The Holy Spirit softly whispered, "You never felt like you were anyone's baby." Just as He'd given the revelation, He quickly shared; you were God's baby, even before you were in your mother's womb." I think this is why I was so partial to the verses in Romans 8. God foreknew me. He was with me even before the foundation of the world. I was someone special to Him. I just needed to fully understand how special I was.

This lack of understanding made me hungry to be accepted. I had always been the clown in the bunch. God later revealed that it was my need for attention; to be noticed, that kept me out front.

48

Folks thought it was a special talent, as it may have been, but it was also a way to mask my true feelings of insecurity and pain.

It wasn't just my past or the ideas I developed in the church, but also many of the things I had been taught throughout my life that framed my behavior. They reinforced the idea that working hard equates to success and self-worth. I'm not advocating being lazy, or nonproductive to achieve success. Commitment, dedication and hard work will typically produce a payoff of some kind. A supernatural outcome, however, starts with, and must be led by Christ. It's all about where you put your trust. You can find what the world defines as success and still have no self-worth. There is a story in the bible that shares the life of Joseph. He was sold into slavery by his jealous brothers. This was only one of many days of trouble he faced, but because the Lord was with him, even in slavery, everything he did was successful!

Genesis 39: 1-3 (KJV)[1] And Joseph was brought down to Egypt; and Potiphar, an officer of Pharaoh, captain of the guard, an Egyptian, bought him of the hands of the Ishmaelite's, which had brought him down thither. [2] And the LORD was with Joseph, and he was a prosperous man; and he was in the house of his master the Egyptian. [3] And his master saw that the LORD

was with him, and that the LORD made all that he did to prosper in his hand.

I've seen a lot of people who have set and reached their goals, but are as empty when they get there as they were before they obtained them. These are people that many would define as successful. I've also seen folks work hard every day toward a goal and in the eyes of other folks, never appear to obtain and yet they had more joy and peace than a man who appears to have it all. Success is dependent on who we perceive to be the source of everything good in our lives and it's not something we fight for, it is a mindset we receive by faith. We are not worthy because of our worth, but Christ's. His never ending love, expressed through grace is why we are eternally successful.

Ephesians 2 8-10 (KJV) [8]For by grace are ye saved through faith; and that not of yourselves: *it is* the gift of God: [9] Not of works, lest any man should boast. [10] For we are his workmanship, created in Christ Jesus unto good works, which God hath before ordained that we should walk in them.

2 Corinthians 5:21 (KJV) For he hath made him to be sin for us, who knew no sin; that we might be made the righteousness of God in him.

Our sinless savior made us forever worthy. Our works could never do what His blood did to cleanse us and make us eternally complete in Him. I truly did not understand this. It's not that I didn't read the scriptures that declared that I had been freed from the law and made righteous in Christ; I just didn't really hear them with my heart. I was definitely looking, just not seeing all the richness that is wrapped up in God's love for me. I was much like the Galatians that Paul speaks to in Galatians chapter three. Though they had received liberty through Christ, they still weren't fully convinced and were drawn away from the truth of the *good news* of Christ, instead trying to demonstrate their own righteousness.

Galatians 3:1-5 (KJV) 3 O foolish Galatians, who hath bewitched you, that ye should not obey the truth, before whose eyes Jesus Christ hath been evidently set forth, crucified among you? ² This only would I learn of you, Received ye the Spirit by the works of the law, or by the hearing of faith? ³ Are ye so foolish? having begun in the Spirit, are ye now made perfect by the flesh? ⁴ Have ye suffered so many things in vain? if it be yet in vain. ⁵ He therefore that ministereth to you the Spirit, and worketh miracles among you, doeth he it by the works of the law, or by the hearing of faith?

Paul asks the Galatians, "Who has fascinated *or* bewitched *or* cast a spell over you...?" He sounds awestruck that even though they had been supplied with the Holy Spirit and seen evidence of God's grace through Jesus Christ, they still fell into their old ritualistic ways. It is all in what you believe to be true.

Have you ever read or heard a story about someone else and thought, "Man, what were they thinking?" I used to wonder as I read about the people in the bible who had access to Jesus and His prophets, how on earth they could not have believed them. Then I remembered that they are not dissimilar from me. I heard about grace and still, somehow, I felt my failures and frailties in life were the result of not meeting some imaginary bar I had set for myself. I didn't recognize that grace is not given based on my goodness, but God's. It's as if we are telling God that the price that Christ paid isn't enough. That's what we're really saying when we start trying to make deals with God by our works in exchange for the things we need and want. Somehow, we begin to think we can affect the outcome with our own efforts so we abandon our faith and start handling things ourselves. It's not that your faithful service to your family or the church is wrong. Believe me, most churches desperately need committed workers and I pray that you will be counted in that honored number. I also pray that the motivation for your work, even if your teaching or preaching is to the glory of God and not to prove to yourself or others that you are worthy of God's blessings. The desire that I had to be more pleasing to God was even more urgent for me if I knew I had done something that I felt was wrong. In fact, I was so focused on my efforts, even if I couldn't remember doing anything wrong, I began to question if I had somehow failed or missed what God wanted. Maybe, I imagined, whatever uncomfortable situation I was in was the result of my failure. This is what happens when you are still living under the law of sin and death instead of the law of grace. I was sin conscious, not God conscious.

It is very dangerous to judge God based on our situations. He is not like men who are ruled by their feelings. God doesn't need to send a tornado to show us our need for Him; He sent the law and it became very evident we needed a savior. Then He sent a savior. That was enough. We'll talk about this a bit more in later chapters. What you need to be assured of is that an intimate relationship with God will place you in a position to hear the urgings of the Holy Spirit. If the Holy Spirit pricks your heart that you are in sin, a change of mind (repentance) is the best answer for sin. Once you have a change of heart, your actions will follow suit. Your frailties are not a surprise to God, they were very apparent to Him. That's why He put a plan in place before the world was ever created to send a savior to redeem you from your sins. It may sound strange, especially to those of us who feel we've worked for everything we've ever obtained, but in God, the work is in believing. We've been called to believe that we were justified by Christ.

Acts 13:38-39 (KJV) [38] Be it known unto you therefore, men and brethren, that through this man is preached unto you the forgiveness of sins:[39] And by him all that believe are justified from all things, from which ye could not be justified by the law of Moses.

I could read the scriptures, even quote them, but I wasn't completely free. I took part of the word, and part of a lifestyle I had become accustomed to. My efforts became a way of self-medicating. I felt less helpless and alone in my situations if I was doing something to change them. I didn't fully understand the power of fighting the good fight of faith rather than waging war on my own. I also didn't completely understand that I was never alone because my God would never, never forsake me! This is something I know I didn't have knowledge of, because I was painfully lonely for years. Thankfully, one of the things that did come from my pain was pause. Not rest. Rest is only possible when you're fully trusting God. Unfortunately, I was pausing from exhaustion. My efforts and the overwhelmingly painful situation I was in finally brought me to the end of myself. I was no longer running every which way as I had been for years. I was no longer using *my* resources, patience, and strength. Finally, in this place of absolute brokenness, after many years of mixing a reliance on God with self-reliance, I was ready to really hear God. Oh and the things I began to hear from God now that I was really listening.

CHAPTER 3

LOVE LIFTED ME

The love of God is a force with supernatural capabilities that render even the toughest opponent powerless. It is impossible to truly experience God's agape love and not be better for it. I have often said; if you nag and pressure someone long enough, you may impact their behavior, but the love of God can do more than that, it can transform their heart.

The love relationship that God desires to eternally share with us is amazing. You would think that receiving it would be the easiest thing for us to do. Unfortunately, for many of us, by the time we are introduced to God, we've already spent far too much time getting acquainted with the world's definition of love. It is no wonder that so many people have a difficult time with the concept of God's love. For many people, love has been an empty, conditional phrase that is all too casually spoken, but often falls far short of our expectation of it. The definition of love that most of us are familiar with is "an intense feeling of deep affection." The problem with this love is that it is typically conditional and based on circumstances that are subject to change. We get older, or become sick, or have emotional issues, or lose our finances or homes, or other resources and for some folks, this is enough to change the way they feel about us. Additionally, there are so many folks who have been caught up in unfortunate situations where the words were spoken, but it was never demonstrated. I have met so many young people out on the streets who left homes of abuse where the words of love were spoken by drug addicted or violent parents, but the demonstration was not deep affection. This resulted in the wrong idea about what love is and how it is demonstrated. That is why surrendering to God's love is sometimes such a challenge. We equate the word love with our knowledge of it and it is often painful.

The word love appears in the bible many times, but can actually be translated into four different meanings depending on the use of the word. For most of us, love has presented itself in so many forms by the time we are introduced to God's love; it makes His love seem unbelievable. Before I truly received God's love, I had been *loved* before and I had the scars to prove it. These scars were a constant reminder of pain, not promise. They reminded me of the failed relationships I had both witnessed and been a part of. They also reminded me that there was a price to pay for giving your heart to someone else. I was capable of loving, but not the way God desires us to love. This is only possible after you have received pure love from the God that is love. I thought I was clear on what it meant to be in love and to be loved, but I don't believe I had ever really experienced either. This is not the fault of those around me, we all do what we know best to do.

We can find no greater expression of love than the selfless sacrifice of our savior, Jesus Christ who demonstrated love as He took our place of punishment for sin on the cross.

What is True?

Of the four words that translate in the English word for love, only one, agape, represents God's perfect love. Agape is selfless, unconditional love. The other words, though translated as love, do not mean perfect love. They are eros which is sensual or sexual love like that between a man and wife, phileo which is a close friendship or brotherhood, and storgay which is family love like that shared between a mother and her child. We are likely most familiar with the other demonstrations of love; eros, phileo and storgay. The challenge with only having experienced these forms of love, is that they are conditional and based in most cases on our feelings. Because our feelings can change, it is also possible for our demonstration of love to change. This explains how someone you care for deeply today, you might despise tomorrow based on some action or thought. It also explains how it is possible for someone to pledge eternal love and then do something that breaks your heart.

Agape love is different. It is unchanging and not based on emotion. It may, in fact go against every emotion you are experiencing. It is not subject to our abilities or characteristics, but does have the power to influence these things. God's agape love can transform us from our fragmented state to a place of healing and wholeness because it is not dependent on us. This love is an indication of God's characteristics, not ours. This means our ability to truly express it requires that Christ be working in us. To demonstrate agape love, we must be selfless.

Based on my prior experiences with love, I never imagined that God's love included provision for me without my works. My life required constant affirmation from others that I was acceptable so I was always doing something. I was involved in almost every auxiliary at my church. I was also often the first at work and one of the last to leave. If it needed doing and made me feel more worthwhile, I did it.

Even with all my laboring, I was focused on how imperfect I was instead of focusing on how good Jesus was. *I didn't really understand that redemption through Jesus was supposed to free me, not bind me.* Some people spend a lifetime trying to receive the acceptance of others when God has already demonstrated that we are eternally accepted through Christ.

You can read the scriptures, but without full comprehension through the Holy Spirit, you limit the power contained in God's word. You have to be able to differentiate the phileo, storgay or eros love we've likely most often received, from the agape love that is God. This is how so many good folks run from God's love instead of running to it. Their ideas of love have all too often been formed by those around them rather than God.

I remember once ministering with several members of my church in an area where homeless families lived. There was a woman there with several children who were clearly living in abject poverty. We found them hunkered under a tree trying to shelter themselves from the rain. Several of her smallest children were piled into a grocery cart that was being pushed by an older child who looked agonized, I presumed, at the way he was living. My heart broke when I saw them. She didn't even have shoes on her feet and I took off the pair I was wearing and gave them to her. Before you celebrate my act of kindness, please know that that was but one side of who I was. I was capable of loving that woman because I overflowed in phileo, but in the next instant, after hearing she might be addicted to drugs, talking about her shamelessly. When I thought of those children living a life of struggle because of her bad choices, all of my compassion for her went out the window. I didn't have any desire whatsoever to help her. I'm not condoning her behavior or the consequences her entire family suffered as a result of it, but I am saying that often we toss people aside when we discover they are not who we envisioned without even a second thought or asking God if we are a part of His plan for their restoration. I am a living testimony, that you can be an amazing worker in God's vineyard, but still be conditional in your love walk. If you are not continuously receiving it, it is impossible to consistently give agape. This means sometimes people get hurt and though it might be hard to admit, we can become both the receiver and the giver of pain.

We have to be so careful what we put our faith in. There are lessons about our world that we've learned from our experience. *Those experiences become our truths and if we're not careful, they replace the real truths God has declared to us in His word.*

I would be remiss if I didn't share that some of the precious people I worked with in churches over the years were among those who taught me that love hurts. This forced me to erect the ever growing wall around my heart. They, like me, may have had a love for God, but because they didn't fully understand His love, they were capable of hurting others. It is possible to develop things you believe around how others treat you. Though I wasn't aware of it, deep down I thought I was only loveable if I looked, felt and acted a certain way. I didn't know I was expecting from God the same things I had received from man; conditional love. People without Christ often base their love and commitment on a set of criteria that if not met will result in rejection. Perfect love does not require that we be perfect. It requires that we believe the sacrifice of love that Christ made on the cross was the perfect atonement for our sins. Through that love sacrifice, we were perfected in Christ.

1 John 4:10 (KJV) ¹⁰ Herein is love, not that we loved God, but that he loved us, and sent his Son to be the propitiation for our sins.

I spent time with God both in prayer and in the Word, but I can't say that the time I spent resulted in a clearer understanding of His love for me. The teaching I received to that point about God's love had deeply established my ideas of who God is. God was a provider, but all too often a punisher of wrong doing and was, in my mind, a distant figure. He was somewhere "out there" in heaven, far too perfect and holy for me to touch. Jesus was "out there" in space, not living inside of me. My old ideas and traditions dulled my perception of what God wanted me to understand and prevented me from the true, meaningful relationship with Him He wanted to cultivate.

To be completely honest, as "holy" as I was, time with God was often a job. My failure to understand Him and His love for me in some ways reduced my relationship with Him down to just another item on my "live holy" check list. There were times when I had meaningful interaction with God, but all too often, I did not. It is impossible to really surrender your time to regular, true fellowship with God and not receive His love and guidance. I could get lost in His presence, but it wasn't long before my mind began to wander to the things I needed to do. I left the place of comfort, love and peace, to *work* so that I could get comfort, love and peace. So many times I felt the tugging to stay in God's presence, but instead moved on to *my* works rather than linger there with Him. This had an impact on my idea of His love and the way it was demonstrated. Had I shared enough time with Him and listened to the urging of His Spirit, I would have fully realized the beauty of His love and that it was far too great for me to ever be capable of earning it. Instead, I stayed just long enough in prayer to confirm to myself that I was acceptable. Rather than linger there, my thoughts typically raced to what I needed to do after I was finished with my "God fix." This of course meant I went to work. There was always a church meeting or event that needed organizing or someone who needed my help, so off I went. How on earth can you work to pay for something that was freely given? *If you are laboring to receive God's love, it is an indication that you need a deeper revelation about what it means to be loved by Him.*

Time in the presence of God was still my lifeline, and provided what hope I did have, but it also became another reason for my endless work. Please don't interpret my comments to mean that working for God is not vitally important. There is nothing wrong with pleasing God and He is delighted when our service helps spread the Good News of Christ. My challenge was, while I was committed to doing this, it was not the only motivation for my service. I was convinced that love was best expressed through my actions and through living a perfect life. The problem is, it is impossible for us to produce this kind of life on our own. The Bible declares that everyone has sinned. For me, however, the failure to meet perfection only heightened my feelings of inadequacy. I focused on how to satisfy what I believed to be the criteria for receiving love from God and when I felt I had fallen short, I was certain Gods silence in my life was the consequence. I didn't feel the attachment to God or His love that His word describes; I simply wasn't good enough. If only I had known that God was not only aware of, but had already made provisions for the flawed life I was living. I also didn't understand that it was not my love for God, but His love for me that made me enough in His eyes. *Because I never felt fully connected, it was possible for me to hear about His love in the Bible without experiencing His love.* God is clear in Romans 8:38-39 that nothing can separate us from His love; not even our works or our inadequacies.

Romans 8:38-39 (KJV) ³⁸ For I am persuaded, that neither death, nor life, nor angels, nor principalities, nor powers, nor things

present, nor things to come, [39] Nor height, nor depth, nor any other creature, shall be able to separate us from the love of God, which is in Christ Jesus our Lord.

My daughter and I spent countless hours shopping when she was younger and of course we had to bring along my son. It was truly one of the things she and I enjoyed doing. Mall therapy became another coping mechanism for me and I felt, based on all of my long-suffering efforts with those I served, I deserved to spend money. It is funny how many excuses for our behavior we can come up with when we want to.

My son, who was the youngest, made every trip to the mall an adventure. He would disappear under wracks of cloths and then suddenly reappear frightening us as he did. He would wander off and I would have to stop and look for him. It wasn't until I was older and wiser that I realized my poor little boy had been completely bored. He was also very busy.

From the time he could walk I had a hard time keeping up with him. His sister had just turned two when he was born and I basically had two babies on my hands. He was the most active child I had ever seen and I admit I invested in one of those child harnesses with the strap (leash) as soon as he could walk. To make matters worse, when I put it on him, he didn't walk calmly at my side. Instead, he stretched himself out to the very end of the harness, leaning as far forward toward the ground as he could go. He looked like a puppy just learning to walk on a leash! It didn't matter how fast I walked, he always wanted to get wherever we were going faster than I could go. I remember folks used to stare at us when I took him out in public, but the advantages of using the harness far outweighed any embarrassment! The alternative would have been to lose my child. He delighted in running from me and making every event an opportunity for play! This would have been fine if we lived in a world where everyone was trustworthy and had his best interest at heart. Regrettably, this was not our world. The idea of losing him to someone who would harm him was beyond what I could bear, so I put a harness on him so that I could assure that he stayed close to me. It wasn't just for me, but also for him. He would have been very upset after he tired of his game and realized I was nowhere in sight. This is exactly what our God did. The thought of forever losing the love relationship He created us to share with Him was unacceptable. Even though Adam's sin separated us from God in the Garden of Eden, God wanted us to have the opportunity to have fellowship with Him and experience His everlasting love for eternity. I didn't understand this because I was busy trying to analyze the words and not the message in the Word of God.   The result was that I was in love with God, but not convinced of His love for me. There is no way to understand God's love for us using human reasoning because it simply doesn't make sense. When most of us consider what we have learned about love from those around us, it's hard to think that God could truly love us and demonstrate that love unconditionally.

In the book of Ephesians, Paul's prayer indicated the people in Ephesus too needed to have a deeper understanding of God's love.

Ephesians 3:17-19 (KJV) [17] That Christ may dwell in your hearts by faith; that ye, being rooted and grounded in love, [18] May be able to comprehend with all saints what is the breadth, and length, and depth, and height; [19] And to know the love of Christ, which passeth knowledge, that ye might be filled with all the fullness of God.

True Love

Agape love requires supernatural understanding to comprehend and we need the power of the Holy Spirit to lead us into the truths concerning it. *Without the benefit of a consistent spiritual guide, my thinking didn't always line up with God's.*

You would presume that a life changing situation such as divorce would make you more keenly aware of God's love, but for me it only magnified my feelings of being unlovable. The process of divorce brought with it strong feelings of rejection. I was convinced that not only was I not good enough for my husband, but for anyone. I looked at myself and began to evaluate everything about me; I was too fat, getting old; to unyielding, undesirable. The list of my flaws was long. I was thankful that God loved me at all, but ran to His love in desperation, not assurance. The more imperfect I felt, the less I felt loveable by anyone, even God. The fact that I had been taught lessons that implied that God's love was conditional only heightened my feelings of inadequacy and unworthiness. This is the result of living by the rigidity of the laws that Moses received from God instead of living by the power of grace through Christ. You will never be able to be that perfect person the law requires on your own and the more you fail, the more unlovable you feel. We cannot forget that God is all knowing. The Bible shares with us that He is the beginning and the end. He's already seen into eternity and there is nothing that we have done or ever will do that is a surprise to Him. He loved us *first*, unconditionally, and will love us eternally. God is not just a superpower with the ability to demonstrate some of the characteristics we associate with love. God is Love! He not only knew of our frailties, but made provisions for them.

Romans 5:7-8 (KJV) [7] For scarcely for a righteous man will one die: yet peradventure for a good man some would even dare to die. [8] But God commendeth his love toward us, in that, while we were yet sinners, Christ died for us.

God's love is not a response to who we are, but a reflection of who He is. I was finally realizing this. Faced with this new revelation about God, I had to choose to receive His truth in place of the misconceptions I had believed.

We only have to remember the act of love that took place on the cross to understand how agape love is demonstrated. Jesus Christ, who is Life itself, endured persecution and crucifixion, though He had the power to live in spite of the destruction of His physical body. He chose, for our sake to live through the pain of crucifixion and then finally surrender His physical body so that we might live.

John 3:16 (KJV) [16] For God so loved the world, that he gave his only begotten Son, that whosoever believeth in him should not perish, but have everlasting life.

Isaiah 53:4-5 (KJV) Surely he hath borne our griefs, and carried our sorrows: yet we did esteem him stricken, smitten of God, and afflicted. [5] But he *was* wounded for our transgressions; *he was* bruised for our iniquities: the chastisement of our peace *was* upon him; and with his stripes we are healed.

What a tremendous price to pay for you and me. How valuable we must be! Anything less than receiving the full measure of God's wrath would have made Christ's sacrifice incomplete. As horrific as the beatings were and the unimaginable suffering His body must have endured as they crucified Him, it wasn't until He paid for the full extent of our sins that He could declare, "It is finished." These simple words and the acts that preceded them though brutal, reflect the price that was paid for our peace. They also express the beauty of Gods unconditional love for us. Jesus' torture and death did not occur because we were great, or perfect, or even holy, but because of God's greatness and eternal love for us. I can't say this enough; our righteousness is not something we've earned, but something that was given to us, in spite of us!

I have heard that the nails that pierced Him were likely between seven and nine inches long. It wasn't the nails, however that held our Savior to the cross; they could not have kept Jesus, because they were never holding Him there. Love held Him to the cross and the same love brought Him up from the tomb to be seated with God; love for us. I had searched all my life for someone who would "love me right." Finally, I had found Him. My answer was in Jesus! If what Jesus did isn't the greatest demonstration of love, I don't know what is.

I thought back to times in my life when I actually imagined that God loved other people differently than He loved me. I was sure it had to do with their work or position. I used to imagine, the Pastor was able to do more because God favored him differently and loved him more. He has more time to spend with God, I thought, and so God has a different love relationship with him. I didn't consider that time spent with God equated to intimacy and created the confidence my pastor demonstrated in Him. Instead, I thought spending time with God was a display of worthiness for which you got a reward. People, I presumed, who God felt were more worthy of His favor and love received more of His generosity. This isn't true. God is not a respecter of persons like man is.

Acts 10:34-35 (KJV) 34 Then Peter began to speak: "I now realize how true it is that God does not show favoritism 35 but accepts men from every nation who fear him and do what is right.

Power to Overcome

There are people in my church that just seem to overcome things no matter how difficult. These folks know how to encourage others even when they are going through unthinkable situations themselves. They have tapped into the love of God and understand the empowerment they have received because of grace.

I remember when my Pastor's mom died. He was obviously very saddened by her death, but rather than shut himself in at home, he actually came and taught at our church. I marveled as I watched him speak just a few days after she passed away. He was clearly affected by her passing, but he wasn't hopeless or helpless. He had not chosen to allow her death to make him a victim. He had chosen instead to remain victorious and allow God's joy to be his strength. I used to sing a song called "Love Lifted Me." There was something wonderful about the idea that love had the ability to lift me up out of my situations. I saw in my Pastor's demonstration of courage in the midst of great challenges, the love of God at work. He was truly lifted beyond his circumstances. His living testimony of strength made me hungry for what he had.

My pastors have taught me many love lessons from both their teaching of God's word and their lives. It was the way they walked out God's love that ultimately captivated me. I became a faithful member of Living Word International Church because of the God in them.

I confess I entered this church suspicious of everyone, but the power of love overtook my doubts and quieted my fears. We have to realize what a powerful force love is. It gives us the ability to open the doorway to abundant life for ourselves and if we demonstrate that force in the liberty God has given us, it also transfers to others.

I had been wrestling to make sense of the season I was in, being connected once again with a spiritual family was critical for me. I mentioned earlier that just as I was dealing with divorce; I was also dealing with giving up our small church. It is hard to describe the devastation I felt. I was hurt and confused. I had worked hard in the church, but the work had become only that by the end. I wasn't uplifted or restored, just busy. I was so busy that I didn't even recognize that the efforts of the church became a ritual and mechanical and no longer represented good fruit. It was time to shut the church down. I felt angry that it had taken me so long to realize I was working without the benefit of the

Holy Spirit. Once I was through with the church, I didn't trust the church environment anymore. I decided to take a break from any church services. My anger should really have been directed at my own actions. I had allowed my need for justification to override God's desire for me to effectively share His word. In my attempts to please God, somehow, I began to do things without Him. My love walk was all messed up too. With all of that going on, I felt like I was divorcing my husband and the church.

Thankfully my pain didn't keep me away from church long. I still knew where my help would come from and I needed to get myself back in fellowship. I had attended church all of my adult life, primarily working as a servant in it. After a few months, even though I was feeling confused and sorry for myself, I began visiting a few churches, and finally felt the leading of God to join Living Word. In this wonderful place, I was introduced to Pastors Edward and Patricia Thomas. With their help, I underwent a change of heart.

Even with all my years of studying and teaching the word, my mind needed to *be transformed by the renewing of the word.* There were truths that I had simply never heard, at least not with the full benefit of the Holy Spirit; the Spirit of Truth. I had valuable skills to offer the church, but not in the condition I was in. My soul was wounded. Pastor Thomas often used to say, "Hurting people hurt other people." This was me. By the time I arrived at the church, I was at an all-time low. I was overly critical, sometimes too judgmental, and didn't trust anyone. Feelings of inadequacy have an effect on how we see the world and ultimately the type of love walk we display. I saw the world, but it was as if I had on a pair of tainted glasses and they made my response to it a guarded and suspicious one. As I grew in the knowledge of God's love, I looked back at my Pastor's acceptance of me and realized that they had never passed judgment on me. I came to know them as powerful people of faith who genuinely expressed unconditional love. There was no greater demonstration of their faith in God than the humility with which they served and loved others, regardless of how fragmented people were. I was sure they recognized that I was, at times, responding through my pain. I felt they must have seen that my wounded heart had compromised my ability to consistently love with the love of God. This was not the case. Because they were filled with the love of God, it was as if they didn't have the ability to see my faults, only what God created me to be. They constantly spoke abundant life into me and their words and the word of God they presented to me encouraged and empowered me to be better. This is what our Heavenly Father sees as well. Christ's sacrifice

77

gave us an eternal entitlement to God's righteousness by faith. When He sees us, He sees Himself. The more I knew that, the more I began to love me too. If God Almighty could love me that much, surely I could love myself.

I started spending more time meditated on that truth, and began to realize that I was valuable. Love is the weapon God has given us that works most effectively against the powers of our adversary. Not our love, but His. When we comprehend how much we're loved by the Father, we can receive His word as our final authority. In knowing this, you must also know that because it is such a powerful weapon, it is always under attack. There is a constant war being waged against agape. The accuser carries on a continuous effort to discredit, devalue, and wreak havoc in our love walk by pointing out all of the flaws of those God has sent us to love and serve. At the same time he's lying to us, he's also lying to those around us, but God has provided a way out and His name is Jesus Christ. He is our truth! We no longer have to walk in condemnation, nor do we have to condemn others to elevate ourselves.

Romans 8:1-4 (KJV) [1] There is therefore now no condemnation to them which are in Christ Jesus, who walk not after the flesh, but after the Spirit. [2] For the law of the Spirit of life in Christ Jesus

hath made me free from the law of sin and death. ³ For what the law could not do, in that it was weak through the flesh, God sending his own Son in the likeness of sinful flesh, and for sin, condemned sin in the flesh: ⁴ That the righteousness of the law might be fulfilled in us, who walk not after the flesh, but after the Spirit.

The *law* I was basing my worth on, was powerless to provide me with the life I prayed for. I was so familiar with this "law of sin and death" that I thought I had to live by it, not fully understanding that I had been redeemed from its requirements. The cost for my sin was paid through the death of Jesus Christ, the Son of God. *The cross is the evidence of God's uncompromising love toward us regardless of our failures.*

If you look closely, John 3:16 contains our instructions for how to enter this eternal love relationship with God. This scripture clarifies that it was God's love alone that prompted Him to give His precious son. It doesn't require years of mindless work to show our worth. What is required is that we allow the Holy Spirit to translate the heavenly language of love in a way that we can believe and receive it. God expressed His unconditional love for us by sacrificing His son in our place to pay the price for our sin.

Cease From Your Labor and Receive Love

When we receive God's love and acceptance, we can allow ourselves to stop working to obtain righteousness and enter into the place of rest that was afforded to us because of Jesus' death. His atonement for our sins paid a debt we could never repay and released us from an old covenant that required us to work to demonstrate our righteousness. Now we can rest in the assurance that the gift of God's love was enough. This gift was Jesus Christ who has given us the ability to truly cease from our works and receive His finished work on the cross.

Matthew 11:28-30 (KJV) [28] **Come unto me, all ye that labour and are heavy laden, and I will give you rest.** [29] **Take my yoke upon you, and learn of me; for I am meek and lowly in heart: and ye shall find rest unto your souls.** [30] **For my yoke is easy, and my burden is light.**

In Luke the sixth chapter Jesus declares to a group of judgmental Pharisees that He is the Lord of the Sabbath. Sabbath comes from the Hebrew word Sabat which means to rest or cease from labor. Though these men did not understand the full meaning of Jesus' purpose that day, what He was trying to communicate is that He was the Lord of rest. With His coming, a time of living by a new commandment of love was being ushered in, to replace the season of work that the law required. Thousands of years later, so many folks still don't comprehend that the season of working to obtain God's acceptance and love is over. Now instead of having to shoulder the weight of our cares, by trusting in Christ, we cast our cares on Him.

We can gladly take His yoke with the assurance that He will lead us where we ought to go. Though not visible, this yoke is a harness of sorts similar to the one I strapped on my son to assure that nothing would separate him from my love and care. We are invited to take on this yoke in place of the ones we have carried in our self-reliance. In so doing, He ensures that we don't come into harm's way and that we are eternally close to Him. There is something supernatural that happens when we leave the burden of our work and take on Jesus' rest, allowing Him to lead. As long as we try to work, pulling to go our own way, we'll never enter into the rest that is such a powerful indication of His love.

Love will cause you to trade your burdens for God's endless resources. I used to read about this yoke that God desired to place on me. Receiving this yoke was much like what I imagine my son must have felt with that harness wrapped on him. Like him, I wanted to go further, faster than God would sometimes allow. When I used to envision a yoke, I imagined it was something binding, restricting; not guiding and leading to abundant, still waters of life. Appreciating the heart of God helps us understand the safety that can be found in the yoke He desires for us to receive.

The Measure of Real Love

As I began to accept God's love, it also enabled me to receive His yoke in place of the yoke of bondage I had been wearing for far too long. My stinking thinking almost cost me the greatest love affair ever given to man.

So many people measure God's love by their circumstances. If their walking in abundance; God really loves them. If they're in poverty, or sickness; God must surely be unhappy with them or angry because they don't feel His love. God is not like that; if He made a promise to you, He will surely do it!

Numbers 23:19 (KJV) God *is* not a man, that he should lie; neither the son of man, that he should repent: hath he said, and shall he not do *it*? or hath he spoken, and shall he not make it good?

We are made complete when we run to God, not when we pull away from Him. If you are convinced, like I was, that you have to be loveable to be loved, go back and see for yourself. This was not a requirement of the love covenant God gave us with His only son. Remember when we receive love, we receive God because God is Love. He is not just the characteristics of love that are so eloquently described in 1 Corinthians 13.

1 Corinthians 13:4-7 (KJV) [4] Charity suffereth long, and is kind; charity envieth not; charity vaunteth not itself, is not puffed up,[5] Doth not behave itself unseemly, seeketh not her own, is not easily provoked, thinketh no evil;[6] rejoiceth not in iniquity, but rejoiceth in the truth; [7] beareth all things, believeth all things, hopeth all things, endureth all things.

As I allowed myself to be transformed, I realized that the Bible is a love story. It contains demonstration after demonstration of God's love for us. Many of the precepts I had read for years began to jump off the pages and into my heart with brand new meaning. God wasn't the impersonal prosecutor I had always envisioned Him to be. God was the truest definition of a friend, a father, a leader, a confidant, a provider that I could ever know. He was the God of true hope, mercy and kindness who had put a tremendous amount of effort into assuring that I had full access to His eternal love. When I finally accepted that, I began a real love relationship with Him. I didn't just love Him as some distant deity who had the ability to love or withhold love from me depending on my works. He became the real source of every promise He had made. As certain as Gods love was for me, that's how certain I became that He not only could, but desired to do all that He had promised. The love affair that I entered into with God was so much deeper and richer than anything I previously experienced. Now I no longer had any fear that my imperfections would drive Him away or make Him be unkind. What I had experienced from so many other people who professed to love me, I had projected on God.

I had had relationships and friendships with people, but some of them, taught me lessons in pain and mistrust, not in true love. These experiences with love framed my beliefs and I was horrified that God would one day reject me and walk away too. What would I do without Him? I knew enough to know that He was ultimately my only hope and without Him I would surely be lost.

Never use the measuring stick of your experience to define God. The love of man cannot compare to the perfect love we receive from God. There was something very liberating about falling for someone who has and will always love you. I felt fixed in areas of my life that I didn't even know were broken. The world looked different when I saw all of the things that were possible instead of the things that were not. Understanding I was now unconditionally loved was the evidence I needed to truly believe I was also justified in Christ without my endless efforts. I replaced my book of "shalt not's" with a new truth; "all things are possible to those who believe." Lord, I believe!

1 John 4:16 (KJV) [16] **And we have known and believed the love that God hath to us. God is love; and he that dwelleth in love dwelleth in God, and God in him.**

CHAPTER 4

HIS GRACE IS SUFFICIENT

When I received God's love I had a new level of trust and understanding for His word. The relationship I was building with Christ also made me want to spend more time getting to know Him. The more I read about His goodness and all of the provisions He had put in place just for me, the more I felt admiration and real love and trust for Him. I had read the bible, but I started to realize that absent from the intimate relationship I was beginning to share with God, I had missed some of the most life changing concepts. Among the ideas I had misinterpreted was the idea of God's grace. I had been taught that it was His unmerited favor, but for what? What was this grace for? What did that really mean to me and how did that compare to the concepts I had been taught that were based on the early laws God's people lived by before Christ came to the earth? I never stopped to ask myself any of these questions before because I assumed I already knew what I needed to know. I did not consider that even my interpretations of the bible could be influenced by the glasses of skepticism I sometimes wore.

If we read the bible without seeing the person of Christ in the words, it is just an interesting book. We can never separate the love relationship God shares with us from His word. That relationship puts a real voice to the letters and takes us from logos to rhema. The word logos is a Greek word and simply means "word." When you read the logos (word) of God, you are reading the bible the way you would a text book to obtain knowledge about a specific topic. Rhema, though it is also translated to mean "word," is more than just the written word. When you receive rhema, it is orchestrated by the Holy Spirit. The word, presented to us in this way, becomes more personalized. It is like we are invited to leave the general classroom for a private tutoring session with God and He speaks truths to us that move the words beyond just knowledge of who God was as a historic figure. Through the rhema word, we receive a personal revelation of who God is as Abba Father and who Christ is as Lord and Savior. The words seem to somehow come to life and leap from the pages. This kind of experience can occur when you are in private study or in the middle of a stadium of people hearing someone teach. The focus is not just on the physical location, but the spiritual atmosphere in which you receive the word of God that makes all the difference.

I realized too often, I was not receiving the meat of the word. This meant I was being sustained by what I knew and even to some degree, blessed by it, but there was not enough substance in it to completely transform me. I could be cold and then hot; excited and in great anticipation one day about the direction of my life then discouraged and hopeless the next. Of course this is an oversimplification of my reality. I could go a while on what I knew, but after my efforts didn't bring the fruit I expected, I would gradually slip into doubt and discouragement. Apart from the rhema word, you can hear the word, but not receive it with faith. This makes the word of no effect.

Hebrews 4:2 (KJV) ²For unto us was the gospel preached, as well as unto them: but the word preached did not profit them, not being mixed with faith in them that heard it.

The word is supposed to be a living power that has the ability to change our thinking and beliefs to the degree that even the intangible becomes possible. If you're only hearing it, like you would a good storybook, you may be able to sustain yourself, as I did, but you have to ask yourself if that is the abundant and fulfilling life God promised you.

I was praying one day in my car on the way to work and asking God about an issue. It was something I was aggravated about and I felt I already knew the answer. This, by the way, was how I ended up in such a fragile state in the first place; assuming that I knew the heart of God based on *my* knowledge, interpretation of His word, and experiences, rather than actually seeking the heart of God for my circumstances. In any event, this particular day, I was driving along, sharing my solutions for this challenge with God when suddenly I saw an image in my mind. In this image, I was looking for something in the refrigerator because I was hungry. A leftover piece of pizza immediately caught my eye and I quickly grabbed it, ate it and went on about my day. I saw myself later reaping the fruits of that piece of pizza and believe me they were not fruits that I desired. As I absorbed these images in my mind's eye I was also talking to God and noticed that I was drawn back to the refrigerator. Further back on the same shelve was a beautiful salad. It was fresh and filled with everything I needed. I saw vegetables, and meat, and fruit and cheese. Of course, I had no appetite for the salad at that point; I was already having a reaction to the pizza. God was showing me that I can choose to find a solution, even one in His word, that will satisfy my desires, but there is a richer, deeper solution. This solution will ultimately bring about His best if only we will dig a little deeper.

We can quickly move to the letter of the word and while it may provide some nourishment, if we want the power of transformation that renews our mind, we have to allow the Spirit of Truth to be our guide and not *our* truths. It is possible to make the Bible say whatever you need to try and get what you *want*, but that doesn't mean it will give you what you *need*. Our God promised to supply all our needs, not all the crazy things we think we want! I thank Him that there were times He did not answer my prayers!

Philippians 4:19 (KJV) ¹⁹ But my God shall supply all your need according to his riches in glory by Christ Jesus.

I love that He will supply according to His glorious riches. No matter what our interpretation of God's Word is, He's not going to simply fulfill it with junk. It is out of His glorious riches He will make Himself known to us.

Had I been in the position to comprehend what grace truly meant for me, I would have been able to find my way out of the discouragement and shame I ended up in. I would have discovered deeper roots in God. Thank God His mercy provides sustenance, but His grace has given us access to so much more!

For so many years I mixed the stories I heard and read in the Old Testament with the information I was being given about God's grace. I read that Christ came to fulfill the law. *To me that meant we were still subject to everything that was a part of the Old Testament including all of the curses that served as punishment for a less than perfect life.* It is no wonder I was convinced I was a failure. I imagined that God was constantly shocked and disappointment by my shortcomings. Why would I ever think that my weaknesses were a surprise to the one who created me and knew me before He created the world? Jesus even came to earth to live as a man. He had the full consciousness of what it took to be God and to be a man. Who better to serve as our advocate when we need to approach the throne of grace?

Hebrews 4:15-16 (KJV) [15] For we have not an high priest which cannot be touched with the feeling of our infirmities; but was in all points tempted like as we are, yet without sin. [16] Let us therefore come boldly unto the throne of grace that we may obtain mercy, and find grace to help in time of need.

We are encouraged to boldly approach His throne. This scripture in Hebrews is our assurance that who and what we are is not a surprise to our God. In God's mercy, He made a way for our sins to be atoned and His grace came with the power to purify our souls.

I spoke about grace a lot and even shared its meaning with others. "Grace," I would declare," is God's unmerited favor." It is the power to receive every blessing that is available to God's children without having to earn it. With grace comes the ability to do everything that God intended for us when He placed us in the Garden of Eden. We receive this gift by receiving Christ. Our acceptance of His Word as true gives Him a pathway to take up residence in our hearts. I didn't have a problem receiving Christ; the challenge for me was in believing that His unmerited favor was really available to me. I had been taught that Christ came to fulfill the law, but interpreted this to mean that I was still bound to perfectly carry out the old covenant laws. I was not aware that

I was freed from that law which I could never hope to fulfill without faith and was now under a new covenant through Christ.

John 1:17(KJV) [17] For the law was given by Moses, but grace and truth came by Jesus Christ.

The covenant of the law required us to do something good to get something good. I loved God, but could never figure out where I was missing the mark with Him. Surely, I thought, my circumstances were the result of not meeting His criteria. My mind was always conscious of my shortfalls and I was constantly doing something that I thought equated to holiness. I didn't doubt that my works were enough until I came up against a situation where I had to trust God for a long period of time. I would do fine for a bit, but if the season seemed too long and unbearable, I began to consider what I needed to do to get the results I wanted.

The law of grace doesn't require us to do anything except believe that with receiving Christ in our hearts, we've also received the empowerment to go further than the old covenant could ever have allowed. There is such a burden associated with the old covenant. It is a burden that is fueled by fear. Under the old covenant of law, people did not obey God out of love; they did it out of fear of the wrath that would surely come upon them if they did not obey. This was a relationship that was able to achieve God's purpose in revealing to man his sinful nature, but not what He desired for His eternal relationship with us.

In Exodus chapter 24:3 even before the Ten Commandments were given, man entered into a covenant with God where He promised to provide for them in exchange for obedience. This "Book of Covenant" contained instructions for the new nation and required a pledge to obey the new laws. The Children of Israel made a vow to obey all of God's ordinances. This was something that was absolutely impossible for them to do. Our separation from the Creator in the Garden of Eden as a result of Adam's sin made any hope of fulfilling the law apart from God *impossible*. Later, while Moses sought God on Mount Sinai, the people broke their vows to God, constructed a false god and prepared to worship it. God's rage was poured out on them and they quickly learned what it meant to experience God's wrath. Their desire to prove to God that they were self-sufficient instead of God-reliant brought on the kind of suffering they soon began to experience. The law required man to labor to obtain God's provisions, but they found out this was not possible. Regular sacrifices for sin were required to ensure that they did not suffer the wrath of God.

These stories of God's requirements for obedience in exchange for provision were my guidelines for living. I didn't understand the first covenant was established to show man just how futile his efforts were to live a life of holiness without Christ. These early laws communicated by Moses were the set up for the coming King of Kings. Men had to realize their inability to be holy to be willing to receive the source of their holiness. Only then could they be poised to welcome Jesus Christ as their Savior and King. You must first understand you need salvation. If you are not aware you are flawed, you have no desire to be fixed.

At the perfect place in time, God sent His son to be the justifier of His children. This means Jesus stepped forward in the courtroom of heaven's justice and declared that He would pay the price for the sin of man. This act of agape love was done without any assistance from us. It did not require us to be perfect or holy, or even to acknowledge who our Savior was. Before we even knew or were conscious of Him, He was prepared to die for us. Love expressed itself through GRACE. God's unmerited favor on us is the reason Christ offered His body in exchange for ours. The punishment for our sins was death. Jesus, the perfect sacrifice, paid the full price that was required by God to wash away the stain of sin from man.

Galatians 4:4-5 (KJV)[4] But when the fullness of the time was come, God sent forth his Son, made of a woman, made under the law, [5] To redeem them that were under the law, that we might receive the adoption of sons.

Romans 6:23 (KJV)[23] For the wages of sin is death; but the gift of God is eternal life through Jesus Christ our Lord.

The law was the perfect equalizer because every man, regardless of his standing or status transgressed the law. Everyone sinned! This was God's way of demonstrating the need for a savior. The law showed us our frailties and weaknesses, but it could only reflect the image of a man, not change the image. No matter what a man's income or social standing was, the law provided evidence to mankind that we were all sinners in need of a Savior. Jesus sacrifice paved the way for us to be pardoned; forgiven of all of our sins.

Acts 13:38-39 (KJV) [38] Be it known unto you therefore, men and brethren, that through this man is preached unto you the forgiveness of sins: [39] And by him all that believe are justified from all things, from which ye could not be justified by the law of Moses.

Our forgiveness cost an incredible price. Our sin produced an expensive debt that we could have never paid, because we could never have endured the full measure of God's wrath poured out on us as Christ did. His suffering brought our peace and to receive that peace, healing and wholeness, all we have to do is believe. *Acts shares with us that everyone who believes Jesus is their Savior is free and clear, completely justified by His actions on the cross.*

Isaiah 53:5 (KJV) [5] But he was wounded for our transgressions, he was bruised for our iniquities: the chastisement of our peace was upon him; and with his stripes we are healed.

I hope that it is now more apparent why our understanding of God's words and within them the message of grace is vitally important. God sent the perfect sacrifice to pay a debt I could not have paid even if I had tried. Christ has already done what I would never have been capable of doing.

When we do not understand our liberty through Christ, we try to work for our justification. This is what I was trying to do. All my years of dedicated service came from a heart of compassion, but also a heart that was convinced that I was required to work to get the life I wanted. My efforts to be a good wife, mother, employee, minister, were my idea of justification. Strangely enough, the basis for obtaining perfection in these areas wasn't set by God or even those that I was serving, but by me. I am now convinced that that's why I never felt whole. The bar I set for myself to meet before I felt I believed I was acceptable in Christ was an impossible one. I was reading the word of God, but didn't realize that it provided a declaration that my efforts were vain and would not produce the effects I desired. Basically, I was saying to God, "the righteousness you gave me at the cross, your justification, it's not enough. I need to justify myself!" I cringe at the thought that after all that Christ went through for me; I was convinced I still had to do something to be righteous enough to obtain favor in God's eyes.

Strength is Perfected in Weakness

Many of us have been taught that suffering is a source of pride. I sat in many fellowships with Christians where they tried to "one up" each other with their stories of sickness and suffering. I was guilty of it! I had been taught that some things we just had to suffer. I remember hearing about how Paul also was asked to suffer though he pleaded with God to remove the cause of his pain.

2 Corinthians 12:7-9 (AMP) [7] **And to keep me from being puffed up *and* too much elated by the exceeding greatness**

(preeminence) of these revelations, there was given me a thorn (a splinter) in the flesh, a messenger of Satan, to rack *and* buffet *and* harass me, to keep me from being excessively exalted.[8] Three times I called upon the Lord *and* besought [Him] about this *and* begged that it might depart from me;[9] But He said to me, My grace (My favor and loving-kindness and mercy) is enough for you [sufficient against any danger and enables you to bear the trouble manfully]; for *My* strength *and* power are made perfect (fulfilled and completed) *and show themselves most effective* in [your] weakness. Therefore, I will all the more gladly glory in my weaknesses *and* infirmities, that the strength *and* power of Christ (the Messiah) may rest (yes, may pitch a tent over and dwell) upon me!

These scriptures, I thought, were a clear sign that if I was sick, or suffering something Christ had redeemed me from, I should just endure it like Paul. I believed this to be evidence that our sickness, pain and punishment were part of God's plan. I accepted this as confirmation that I would have to endure things that unbeknownst to me I had already been delivered from through Christ. As crazy as it sounds, I believed that my suffering glorified God; that it was a sign of my humility that would bring Him glory. How could God be glorified by allowing affliction to remain upon me when He had already declared that once and for all Jesus bore my sickness and disease on the cross? I am not for a moment implying that those who reign with God will not have to learn endurance through suffering. Endurance strengthens our faith and teaches us truths about God we would never otherwise learn. I am talking about glorifying the situation and staying in it as part of some misguided idea that it brings glory to God, rather than allowing His power to bring you out.

It wasn't until I fully understood the message of grace that I was open to a different interpretation of II Corinthians 12. Though Bible scholars differ on what the thorn represents in Paul's flesh, I tend to agree with the evidence that points to the thorn being the intense suffering he endured as a result of sharing the gospel of Jesus Christ. Paul was stoned and beaten on many occasions and lived to tell about it! Imagine the hostility he must have faced.

2 Corinthians (KJV) 11:23-28 [23] Are they ministers of Christ? (I speak as a fool) I am more; in labours more abundant, in stripes above measure, in prisons more frequent, in deaths oft. [24] Of the Jews five times received I forty stripes save one. [25] Thrice was I beaten with rods, once was I stoned, thrice I suffered shipwreck, a night and a day I have been in the deep; [26] In journeyings often, in perils of waters, in perils of robbers, in perils by mine

own countrymen, in perils by the heathen, in perils in the city, in perils in the wilderness, in perils in the sea, in perils among false brethren; [27] In weariness and painfulness, in watchings often, in hunger and thirst, in fastings often, in cold and nakedness. [28] Beside those things that are without, that which cometh upon me daily, the care of all the churches.

He was once a persecutor of Christians and now because of God's grace was a Christian himself. When Christ declared that His grace was sufficient in 2 Corinthian 12:9, He was declaring that the power Christ gave us at the cross was enough to bring us out of anything the devil could throw at us. He wasn't for a second implying that we should accept our suffering, but rather trust that grace is enough to cover us and see us through it. The trial of our faith gives God the opportunity to demonstrate His love to both us and those around us. Our weaknesses put us in a position to receive God's divine strength. *Jesus does not always remove the situation in the way we want, but will always become the strength to overcome it.*

My son was very small for his age. He eventually had a growth spurt and is now over six-feet tall. When he was little, however, he was small and picked on a lot. He was often teased because of his size, but his sister, if she found out about it, would go crazy to protect him. I once heard a friend of mine say that her brother would declare as they walked onto the playground, "nobody hits my little sister but me!" This is how my kids cared for each other. They would fight constantly, but if one of them faced danger at the hand of someone else, the other raced to their rescue!

One summer, when my son was in elementary school, he had to wait for a bus at a nearby school that took them to another campus for summer school. After several days, my son finally confided in me that while he waited for the bus, he was being hit by a much bigger, older boy. He tried to ignore this kid, but he was a bully, plain and simple. I told his sister and another teen who was staying with us at the time to simply accompany him to the bus stop and inform the boy not to pick on him. My son was horrified that his big sister would be joining him and confronting his attacker, but I insisted. She approached the young man and promptly told him, "If you touch my little brother again, I'll beat you up!" The other teen also assured this kid that hitting on my son would land him a good "butt kicking;" so much for obeying mom. My son was beyond embarrassed. After that, the kid continued to tease him about the incident for a little while, but he didn't touch him again.

My daughter's fierce protection of her little brother is like Jesus, our Savior and Big Brother who sacrificed himself to free us from our attacker. He showed up just in time to stop the abuse we were subject to because of our sin. We may have been small and weak in the eyes of our adversary, but not our big brother! His blood became a sign to the devil that read, "Do not touch!" The devil can taunt and tease us, but he doesn't have the power to destroy us. He will surely try, like the kid who continued to stand at the bus stop and try to intimidate my son. If we resist the devil, we remove any hope of him gaining power over us and he will flee.

Paul rejoiced as he received the knowledge that his infirmities entitled him to the power only Christ could give him. When we are weak, God's unmerited favor has given us access through Christ to supernatural strength. We can tap into the ability to have victory, even in our hard places.

2 Corinthians 12:9 (KJV) ⁹ And he said unto me, My grace is sufficient for thee: for my strength is made perfect in weakness. Most gladly therefore will I rather glory in my infirmities, that the power of Christ may rest upon me.

The Greek word for cover (rest) mentioned in 2 Corinthians 12:9 means to completely shelter or protect something, like a tent keeps us from the rain. Paul received the assurance that rather than simply remove the burden, grace will completely cover it. We are asked not to focus on our weaknesses, but the ability we receive by grace to overcome them. Our limitations are a continued reminder of our need for a Savior. *They are not sent to make us hopeless, but to remind us that our hope should not be in ourselves, but eternally in Christ.*

John 16:33 (KJV) [33] **These things I have spoken unto you, that in me ye might have peace. In the world ye shall have tribulation: but be of good cheer; I have overcome the world.**

The Gift of Freedom

Our adversary, the devil would like for us to believe that the gift of grace did not free us from every curse; that we do not have an entitlement to healing, or prosperity, or any of the other blessings that are now ours. He would love to convince us that we are still guilty. He constantly comes to tell us we are not enough in God's eyes and therefore will be punished. The problem with this is that once you believe it and start to do the work the law requires to be righteous, you also subject yourself to the *consequence* of the law when you fail.

James 2: 10 (KJV) [10] For whosoever shall keep the whole law, and yet offend in one point, he is guilty of all.

Romans 3:19-23 [19] Now we know that what things soever the law saith, it saith to them who are under the law: that every mouth may be stopped, and all the world may become guilty before God. [20] Therefore by the deeds of the law there shall no flesh be justified in his sight: for by the law is the knowledge of sin. [21] But now the righteousness of God without the law is manifested, being witnessed by the law and the prophets; [22] Even the righteousness of God which is by faith of Jesus Christ unto all and upon all them that believe: for there is no difference: [23] For all have sinned, and come short of the glory of God;

There is no possible way that we could ever receive God's blessings under the law because all of us are sinners. If perfection, which the law requires, is the basis for blessing we will never be eligible for them! This is why man had to repeatedly offer up a sacrificial lamb for the atonement of his sin.

Romans 3:23-28 (KJV) [23] For all have sinned, and come short of the glory of God; [24] Being justified freely by his grace through the redemption that is in Christ Jesus: [25] Whom God hath set forth to be a propitiation through faith in his blood, to declare his righteousness for the remission of sins that are past, through the forbearance of God; [26] To declare, I say, at this time his righteousness: that he might be just, and the justifier of him which believeth in Jesus. [27] Where is boasting then? It is excluded. By what law? of works? Nay: but by the law of faith. [28] Therefore we conclude that a man is justified by faith without the deeds of the law.

Receiving by faith God's gift of grace is an admission that we are made righteous because God is righteous. It has absolutely nothing to do with us; therefore, we can't take credit for it. All of the glory goes to God.

Ephesians 2:8-9 (KJV) [8] For by grace are ye saved through faith; and that not of yourselves: it is the gift of God: [9] Not of works, lest any man should boast.

I have worked for several years in management. While I would consider myself a very liberal manager, thankfully, the folks I work with respect the role I have to play. If I'm in a closed-door meeting, they don't simply barge in. I have from time to time received a text message asking for access into a closed door meeting, but typically, they do not interrupt me unless it's an emergency. My daughter, on the other hand, when she was a student at the university I worked at, would knock on the door to my office and quickly open it. She would announce what she came to get or use, and come right in. This didn't bother me, nor did I feel it was a sign of disrespect. I was a busy professional and minister and my children often had to share my time with others. Still, they were clear that because of our relationship, they had full access to me. That relationship gave them access that others did not.

It is the same way with our Heavenly Father. When Adam ate the forbidden fruit in the garden, he immediately became aware of his sinful nature. This nature placed a wedge between him and God. He no longer had the access to God he once had. The consequence of Adam's sin was death or separation from God.

Christ removed that wedge, but the devil continuously tries to remind us of that sinful nature. He would have us believe that we are under condemnation and still held captive because of our sins to the confines of the law.

Romans 8:1-8 (KJV) There is therefore now no condemnation to them which are in Christ Jesus, who walk not after the flesh, but after the Spirit. ²For the law of the Spirit of life in Christ Jesus

hath made me free from the law of sin and death. [3] For what the law could not do, in that it was weak through the flesh, God sending his own Son in the likeness of sinful flesh, and for sin, condemned sin in the flesh: [4] That the righteousness of the law might be fulfilled in us, who walk not after the flesh, but after the Spirit. [5] For they that are after the flesh do mind the things of the flesh; but they that are after the Spirit the things of the Spirit. [6] For to be carnally minded is death; but to be spiritually minded is life and peace. [7] Because the carnal mind is enmity against God: for it is not subject to the law of God, neither indeed can be. [8] So then they that are in the flesh cannot please God.

He wanted me to come out from under the confines of the law and receive the new covenant and abundant life. This life offers continuous access to the endless resources of heaven and even more importantly, our Heavenly Father. Our access to these resources is how we produce works of the Spirit.

I was emerging as a new creature. As the Holy Spirit began changing my mind, I started to realize just how much my old ideas had kept me captive to the fleshly man. This was the part of me that ultimately wanted what it wanted and it is likely why I stayed on the rollercoaster of emotions that was my life. I was in a world of pain and trouble while ministering to others. Looking back, I don't remember even asking God about some aspects of my life. I would read His word or heard His word preached in a certain way, felt I had received it, and thought I was living it. I decided what I was doing was in line with His commands so why ask for direction? God shares that "we have not because we ask not." There were areas in my life that were not yielded to the Holy Spirit because I was convinced based on my interpretation and my knowledge that I was walking upright. We have a responsibility to hear what the word of God is saying by the Spirit of Truth. It will lead us and guide us into all truth. This is something we can never achieve on our own; it is a continuous act of faith in God as the source and not we ourselves.

What do you do when you hear something that challenges your old thoughts and ideas? In my new church, I was both taught and witnessed numerous demonstrations of the power of grace. Still, in the early days, I was both angry and excited as I learned these new ideas. It didn't matter to me that the concepts I was learning came right from the Bible and had even been broken down from the Greek and Hebrew translations. I confess I did not want to fully receive the message of grace. It sounded so foreign from what I had been taught. I was still learning the message of who

God truly desired to be in my life and about His love for me, and it was just too much to imagine that there was no condemnation for sin. I did not understand that when Christ proclaimed "it is finished," He took the consequence for my sin. Initially, I was confused. Ultimately, this confusion caused me to be hungry for more truth, but at first, it just made me annoyed. I had to discover what the Word was saying. If I had misunderstood what the power of grace truly meant, what else did I need clarity on? The scriptures clearly point to a consequence for disobedience, so how could I be free from the consequence of sin?

Acts 13:38-39 (AMP) [38] So let it be clearly known *and* understood by you, brethren, that through this Man forgiveness *and* removal of sins is now proclaimed to you;[39] And that through Him everyone who believes [who acknowledges Jesus as his Savior and devotes himself to Him] is absolved (cleared and freed) from every charge from which he could not be justified *and* freed by the Law of Moses *and* given right standing with God.

In Acts 13 I discovered my answer. Grace is not a license to sin; it is an entitlement to receive the power that ties us to holiness. It gives us the choice that all men of free will have. We can choose to believe that Christ redeemed us from sin and in so doing connected us to the resources of heaven and God's divine power to live a holy life. We also have the option to cling to the rigidity of a book of rules that is powerless to change us. God is giving us the ability to again walk in the dominion and authority He provided in the Garden of Eden. Receiving the gift of grace also means that we have access to God's guidance by the Holy Spirit. *This guidance will govern our actions and though we might fall into sin, if we continue to believe and seek after God, we can fall into grace.*

I could not believe what I was seeing and hearing. There are so many scriptures in the Bible that talk about the consequences of sin; I really had to dig into what the word says to comprehend this new entitlement. If we choose not to receive Christ as our Savior and rebel against Him, we do not enter into the covenant of grace and are therefore bound to the covenant of the law. This means that we are subject to the consequence of sin or separation from God and the result is the curses so vividly described in the Bible and death. Every punishment that is so vividly pointed out for sinners will come upon those who do not receive the gift of grace. Remember, confessing that you are a believer is not how you obtain your salvation. Believing that you are and receiving Christ as Lord instead of you as Lord is how you are saved.

Gal 2:19-20 (KJV) [19] **For I through the law am dead to the law, that I might live unto God.** [20] **I am crucified with Christ: nevertheless I live; yet not I, but Christ liveth in me: and the life which I now live in the flesh I live by the faith of the Son of God, who loved me, and gave himself for me.**

When Christ chose to lay down His life and die on the cross, His death set men free of the bondage of the law. The atonement for sin that God required under the law was once covered by the sacrifice of animals.   After Jesus Christ became the perfect sacrifice, from that day on, once and for all, our sins were covered by His blood.   When we receive Christ and the work He completed on the cross, we receive the power and authority God gave man in the garden. This is more than enough power, if you truly receive Christ, to live a life that is a reflection of God. By continuing to work as I once did, I was nullifying what Christ did for me.   Look at the Message Bible's clarification of Galatians 2:19-20.

Galatians 2:19-21 (AMP) [19] **For I through the Law [under the operation of the curse of the Law] have [in Christ's death for me] myself died to the Law *and* all the Law's demands upon me, so that I may [henceforth] live to *and* for God.** [20] **I have been crucified with Christ [in Him I have shared His crucifixion]; it is**

no longer I who live, but Christ (the Messiah) lives in me; and the life I now live in the body I live by faith in (by adherence to and reliance on and complete trust in) the Son of God, Who loved me and gave Himself up for me. [21] [Therefore, I do not treat God's gracious gift as something of minor importance and defeat its very purpose]; I do not set aside *and* invalidate *and* frustrate *and* nullify the grace (unmerited favor) of God. For if justification (righteousness, acquittal from guilt) comes through [observing the ritual of] the law, then Christ (the Messiah) died groundlessly *and* to no purpose *and* in vain. [His death was then wholly superfluous.]

I remember once watching a young woman at the altar. She had come up for prayer and repented of her sins and yet for several minutes, almost an hour, she wept inconsolably. The consciousness of her sin had overwhelmed her and she refused to be comforted. Though she'd boldly approached the throne, she could not imagine that just that simply, her desire to change her mind was accepted by God. I shared with her that she was pleading with God to forget about something He could no longer remember. True repentance; a change of heart, is only possible through grace. By grace our sins are covered and all that is seen by God is our righteousness.

Hebrews 8:12 (KJV) "For I will be merciful to their unrighteousness, and their sins and their lawless deeds I will remember no more."

What sin is God referring to? The ones we've already committed? The sins we committed yesterday or this morning? The sins we committed before we were saved? Does He mean all sin? This is what many of us wrestle with. Not believing God meant <u>all</u> sin is how we get into a state of working instead of trusting God. Trusting God opens up a new level of possibilities. This *good news* may be hard to believe, but that doesn't make it untrue! The Word of God is clear.

My heart began to experience a joy like never before. I understood what it meant to be confident in God and not allow every wind of trouble to blow that confidence away.

Hebrews 10:35 (KJV) 35 Cast not away therefore your confidence, which hath great recompense of reward.

Now I was certain I had been made righteous through Christ. Adam's transgression made man subject to the punishment of sin. Christ sacrifice redeemed man from the consequence of sin and restored his authority in the earth. When God saw me, He now saw Himself. The blood of Jesus washed away the stain of my sins and I was again entitled to every blessing God intended in the beginning.

Romans 5:19 (KJV) ¹⁹ For as by one man's disobedience many were made sinners, so by the obedience of one shall many be made righteous.

I began to experience a divine transforming that turned my sadness and insecurity into victory. I no longer felt like I was a perpetual victim. I had declared years ago that we had to choose to be a victim. Unbeknownst to me, my unwillingness to truly seek God's truth had made me just that. Even more than that, as I worked to prove my holiness, I was displeasing God. I was now able to see the irony of giving my life to service unto God's glory without entirely beholding that glory.

My service to God transformed even as my life did. It became a reflection of His promises, not my pain. I had lived so many years fighting to assure myself and others that I was worthwhile, capable and strong; never realizing because of grace, my strength is only made perfect in weakness and total reliance on God as my source.

CHAPTER 5

FAITH EQUALS SUBSTANCE

Settling in at a new church truly blessed me. I was presented with familiar scriptures, but with a new revelation about the love of God, so many of the old passages held new meaning for me. I found myself hungry to know more. The more the word healed my heart, the more I longed for more truths. Still, I was guarded about what some of these new concepts meant in light of what I had held as truths for so long. The more I learned, the more I yearned to fully understand what God was saying in His word. For so long I had been introduced to a God who was a judge and punisher and the idea that He was actually a lover and a close friend really confused me. It challenged some of the things I had been taught up to that point.

If I had been made righteous through Christ where did all my endless labor fit in? I was accustomed to this lifestyle by then and felt awkward and out of place if I wasn't working at some breakneck pace. After all of the years of working and fighting to get acceptance and justification from those around me, I couldn't believe all of that was unnecessary. My life was constructed on a foundation that included working to show my self-worth and my worth to God. I constantly thought about the fact that sin or any act that did not meet God's standard of holiness would result in Him abandoning me. This made all of my suffering acceptable; after all, I thought, like David in the Bible, God could chasten me, but I did not want Him to take His Spirit from me. I mistakenly thought all of the years of hardship and heartache were opportunities to demonstrate my holiness, so rather than use my faith to overcome them; I stayed in them far too long. This is why I gave so much more attention to what I was doing rather than developing a meaningful, lasting relationship with Christ. Had I truly developed it, that relationship would have been instrumental in showing me that it wasn't what I was doing, but what I ultimately believed that kept me bound and in fear.

It caused complete confusion for me as I tried to make the pieces of my law driven life fit with the ideas on grace that I was learning. It was as if the good news of grace was an insult to everything I perceived to be holy. I wasn't aware of it at the time, but my faith had been in my own abilities far more than in the person of Christ who desired to live through me. We guard what we believe to be true about God because it's deeply rooted in who we've become. Over time, we learn how to manage our lives based on these beliefs, even if they are bad. This is why it is so critically important that your faith be squarely rooted in things that can produce the outcome God desires for you. Jesus desires to be our provider. When you trust in things and people who are not capable of providing what you expect, this is how you lose hope, not cultivate faith.

As I began to look back, I discovered that I had not only lost my hope, but my way. Our faith in God's ability through Christ is our passport to the supernatural things God promised us, but first we have to die to what we know and by faith, receive Christ's wisdom.

Gal 2:20 (KJV) [20] I am crucified with Christ: nevertheless I live; yet not I, but Christ liveth in me: and the life which I now live in the flesh I live by the faith of the Son of God, who loved me, and gave himself for me.

Mixed Messages

It wasn't just the idea of changing that challenged me. I had lived so long hearing about sin and the consequences of it, I thought about those consequences a lot. Actually, I was more focused on the punishment of sin and the price I needed to pay to be counted worthy of God's blessings than I was on what the salvation through Christ had made available to me. I was trying to produce abundant life myself, rather than simply receiving it. If you can't believe in the supernatural ability you've been given through Christ, you will never obtain it. This was a really difficult truth after all of the years of being presented with a God who is a punisher. So much of what I learned about God up to that point didn't increase my faith as the bible declares the word should do. In fact, it did just the opposite.

For so many years, I was taught the Ten Commandments and the consequences of sin. This teaching highlighted God's wrath, not His mercy. It is no wonder I found it difficult to understand that it wasn't what I did, but what I believed that made me righteous. The Ten Commandments, without faith, are simply another "to do" list. I was familiar with a "to do" list. What I wasn't familiar with was hearing God's word, hiding it in my heart and thinking on it until it framed my character.

Instead of destroying yokes and removing burdens as the word should do, my early teaching often left me discouraged. The biggest challenge with teaching people to fear God more than you teach them to reverence Him as you receive His love in the person of Christ is that they don't see Him as a resource when they have a problem. When you couple punishment with feelings of rejection and unworthiness like I had, it makes it incredibly difficult for desperate people to truly understand the love of God much less the idea that this love is the evidenced that is needed to have faith in His promises.

We should never equate God's love to a life of punishment for the things we do. If we were truly punished for the things we do, none of us would be here, much less enter into the eternal love God desires to share with us. All of those stern warnings about the consequences of sin for our imperfections turn many people away from God, not encourage them to see Him as a help in their time of trouble. I am not saying that the knowledge of sin and its consequences is not necessary; I'm saying that it shouldn't be a bigger message than salvation through grace. In this message of grace, or the good news is where our power to overcome lies. This message assures us that we don't have to work to be justified, someone far greater than us has already done the work. Our *job* is to believe to the point He did it all and that we can trust His leading toward living a life that reflects His glory.

Since the messages of condemnation were what I had been taught for a long time, the idea that Christ paid for my sin debt seemed unimaginable. I can't reiterate this fact enough because contrary to what so many of us might have been taught, this is the truth. It is a truth that you must believe in order to receive the person of Christ inside of you. Once received, it is the truth that sets you free from the bondage of old ideas, experiences, and traditions. Without this wisdom, you live a life like the one I was living, focusing my attention on myself; trying to be holy enough to be acceptable to God instead of having faith that I was already entitled to redemption from sin. I wanted to look like Christ, but didn't have a full understanding of who He was. Your faith is dependent on your ability to see Christ as the creator of that faith. Hebrews 12:2 reminds us to look unto Jesus, the author and finisher of faith. I heard so many messages that didn't even include Jesus, but rather put an emphasis on what would happen to me if I didn't live a holy life. How can you live a holy life without receiving the Holy One?

Nothing but the Whole Truth

To truly be transformed, I had to commit to not only hearing the truth, but to continuing to hear it. Only then did the word of God take hold of me replacing the confusion I had with clarity. I began to understand that my sins had "once for all time" been atoned through Christ.

1 Peter 3:18 (NIV) 18 **For Christ died for sins once for all, the righteous for the unrighteous, to bring you to God. He was put to death in the body but made alive by the Spirit,**

My failure to see the truths in the word were directly related to my failures. What is interesting to me is that once I saw the truths concealed in the bible, it was almost unbelievable to me that they had been there all along. Do you know it is possible to have knowledge of the word of God, but not have the wisdom to know the truths that are contained in it? The bible is not a publication to simply study as one who is preparing for a test. It is a love letter to those who is seeking a rich treasure. I now knew I was truly forgiven, but thought, surely you must have to do something when you miss the mark with God. How could I be forgiven for things I hadn't even done wrong yet? I reasoned that it must be all wrapped up in how sorry you are for your sins.

When you have been taught that it's not what you believe, but what you do that creates holiness, your life becomes a performance. Even repentance becomes a demonstration of how holy you are; the greater the crime, the greater the need to display to others just how sorry you are. I was reminded of that young woman I had witnessed weeping for so long at the altar. We do so many things to demonstrate our holiness when we don't truly believe we've been made holy through Christ. The demonstration isn't just for others either; often it's for God.

My idea of obtaining God's forgiveness was that I had to lie on the altar, give my best academy award performance before God to show Him just how deeply sorry I was and then try with all my might not to do whatever I had done again. My faith was in my ability. I lived with the sense that I needed to be constantly repentant because I knew it was impossible for me to live a perfect life and I was preoccupied with the consequences of sin. Instead of glad expectation about God, I anticipated the punishment that would surely come if I didn't do exactly what I was supposed to. This pushed me to a life of constantly apologizing for sin, even sin's I wasn't aware of committing. I thought this was the repentance that was required to ensure that I was heaven bound.

God forbid, I would be like those I had heard about who died in a state of imperfection!

I think it is important for us to understand what repentance is. Repentance is not how great our sorrow appears to be when we sin, it is our response to being presented with a truth that overrules the lie we believed that made us sin in the first place. To truly overcome sin, we must repent; or choose to change our minds and in so doing, our lives. Our faith plays a critical part in this process because while revealed knowledge can lead us to change our minds; we have to continue to put our faith in things that are true.

The Greek word for repentance is metanoia. Metanioa means to change your mind. It happens when we discover that past ideas and subsequent actions are wrong. This discovery moves us to change our minds and sometimes brings regret. Regret is not the same as condemnation. The lessons that focused my attention on God's punishment didn't make me more holy. They brought on condemnation that sometimes made me more deceptive. I felt I needed to work harder and harder to appear holy when I missed the mark. You can easily repent when your emotions are touched during a message. That is vastly different from looking into the image of Christ, realizing you are not reflecting that image, and

127

seeking the truths that lead to changing; truths that increase your faith, not diminish it. *Repentance occurs when revealed truth is accepted and empowers us to change our way of doing things to God's way of doing them.*

I believe this is what I was feeling when I finally reached the place of pause that moved me to look deeper at my life to determine the cause of my constant despair. Instead of making excuses for why my behavior was acceptable, or avoiding a more meaningful relationship with Christ, my desperation pressed me to look beyond my walls of fear. It was then that I began to find the courage to except that many of my old ideas, things I had put faith in, were erroneous.

I found, looking back; it had been impossible to overcome my fleshly frailties using my own strength and will, though God knows I tried. Instead of putting all of that effort into convincing myself I was good enough, God's desire was that I cultivate a relationship with Him. He wanted me to learn who He was so that I could trust and believe in not only His ability to do great things through me, but His desire to do them. I started to realize that I had already been freed from the curses – the consequences of being less than perfect. Though this was something the law required; grace gave me the power in Christ to go beyond these commandments. This freedom didn't come by my obedience to the law, but my faith in Christ. This liberty also gave me the confidence to get up and try again when I fell or failed God.

Galatians 3:13-14 (KJV) 1 Christ hath redeemed us from the curse of the law, being made a curse for us: for it is written, Cursed *is* every one that hangeth on a tree: 2 That the blessing of Abraham might come on the Gentiles through Jesus Christ; that we might receive the promise of the Spirit through faith.

Romans 10:4 (KJV)[4] For Christ is the end of the law for righteousness to everyone that believeth.[5]

Ephesians 2:8 (KJV) For by grace are ye saved through faith; and that not of yourselves: *it is* the gift of God:

Only by faith in the finished work of Christ can we truly overcome the obstacles that we are sure to face as we live in an imperfect world. Hearing the Word of God gives us confidence in this work and the ability to have faith in what it accomplished for us.

Until I believed God, I went back and forth, sometimes doing things in my strength and sometimes receiving His strength. Self-reliance is not the same as God reliance. My need to control everything was the strongest evidence that I was walking in self-righteousness and not the righteousness afforded me through Christ. I often said, "If I don't do it, no one will." We become overcomers by faith, not slaves to our fear of the failure of our own devices.

1 John 5:4-5 (KJV) [4] For whatsoever is born of God overcometh the world: and this is the victory that overcometh the world, even our faith. [5] Who is he that overcometh the world, but he that believeth that Jesus is the Son of God?

Enough Faith to Spare

Our faith like our walk in Christ doesn't just impact us, but all of those that God intended for us to reach with the Gospel. If we are spreading fear through the witness of our lives, or our words, we are not advancing the kingdom of God as we were directed to do, but actually hindering the work we were called to do. When our faith is in Christ's ability in us, we have more of a tendency to lead others to the source of our power and not to judge them based on what we perceive to be our accomplishments. I must add here that so many churches are divided, not because of the pastors or even because of the message being taught, but because individuals have not received by faith; the victory that overcomes the world! Faith in action brings heavenly fruit. Fear tears people down and gives birth to division.

More than you can ever imagine, your faith, or lack of it has an impact on the world around you and becomes the greatest testament to who is lord of your life. Many of the great lessons I've learned about faith I have learned from others who have demonstrated it while overcoming incredible obstacles.

There is one individual who stands apart from all of the others. She was a living testament of the power of believing. Her name was Mariah. The times I spent with her will forever be a testimony to what is possible when you tap into the heavenly realm by faith. Over the years I have had the opportunity to know and minister to many children. I have spent years teaching kids in church from ages 2-20. Still Mariah, more than all the others, left an indelible fingerprint of God's love and the power of faith on my heart. Her mother and I have been lifelong friends and we serve as godmother to each other's children. When Mariah was about two years old, her mom began bringing her to my house which had been transformed into a daycare. Mariah was the most spirited child I had ever met. She was the tiniest little thing, but quickly took over the daycare when she arrived each day. I can still see her all buttoned and zipped up in her snow suite with the hood securely tied on her head. Her dad brought her in each morning fastened securely in her car seat and though Mariah loved being with her cousins and the other children at the day care, each morning as she was dropped off, she became angry. I tried everything, along with the other children in my home, to get Mariah to allow me to get her out of that seat and ready for breakfast. She would have none of it. Each day became a new challenge to see how and who would coax Mariah from her car seat. I smile as I remember how much authority she had even then.

Thankfully, Mariah's willingness to fight didn't stop there. She grew older and just before adolescence, went on to battle recurring challenges in her body due to tumors on her brain stem. She fought harder than anyone I have ever seen, but this time, fighting an unwelcome disease in her body while trying to keep those around her calm. She perfected the art of fighting the good fight of faith. I will never forget the day of her first surgery as her family and I walked to the door of the surgery wing. As they wheeled her away for a very dangerous surgery, teddy bear in her arms, she looked back and with a big smile on her face announced, "I'll see you guys in a little while." She continued to smile over the next few years, though she faced health challenges that would have taken the average adult to the brink of giving up. You might wonder how this was possible from a child who would eventually become well acquainted with suffering and pain. Mariah had faith. I know this to be true with every fiber of my being. I watched her do supernatural things beyond the doctor's predictions over and over again because she believed she had the ability to overcome unsurmountable obstacles. She did this with a grace and even a charm that astounded those around her including me. She spent an incredible amount of time in hospitals and specifically in intensive care, but she never lost her spirit or her faith. I believe her faith was not just in the fact that she could beat her illness, but she had faith in God. She had faith in His love for her and I believe she also had faith in her ability to carry out the assignment He had placed on her life.

I remember a particular incident that I feel best describes the faith she demonstrated throughout her life. Mariah was gravely ill and had been flown to a hospital about three hours from our hometown. Her mom had been laboring to care for her in the hospital for several days and was beyond exhausted. I offered to come and relieve her and not long after I arrived, she disappeared for some much needed rest. I sat there passing the time with Mariah who had a large breathing tube in her throat that included tubing that from time to time needed suctioning. She was unable to eat or speak, but could motion if she needed something. I had been sitting with her for quite some time when suddenly, on the loud speaker, I heard an announcement "code blue." I thought for a few minutes about the fact that something serious was unfolding somewhere nearby, but I must be honest and tell you, my first response that day was not to do anything to change the outcome of what I had heard. I didn't even consider it as a cry to move into action, just a normal occurrence in a critical care environment in a hospital. Before I gave it too much thought, I noticed Mariah was motioning wildly at me. I got up and looked at her, in her bed, tubes coming from everywhere, a hole in her throat, fighting for her own life. It took me a few minutes to understand what she wanted me to do. She wasn't beckoning for me to rub her head, as I first thought, or suction her tubing; Mariah was urging me to pray. There she lay as close to heaven as anyone can be on the earth and instead of being concerned about her own wellbeing, she was fully conscious of the need of someone in that hospital for which a distress signal had gone out. Just as I did when Mariah was two and motioning for me to do something before she would allow me to take her from her car seat, I dutifully followed her instructions and prayed. I can't tell you how much I fought tears in that moment. God Himself came

134

to rest with us in that room that afternoon and even as I write about it, I fight tears as I remember the measure of her faith. You see, real faith isn't self-reliant at all, but so confident in God that it empowers those who have it to think beyond their needs to those of others. I drove three hours that day to help a friend and visit my Goddaughter, but that trip did more to demonstrate the concepts God was teaching me about the beauty and strength of our faith than anything I had ever experienced. I realized that faith, like a muscle is strengthened through resistance.

What Do You Know?

What, you might ask, are we resisting? We are resisting the temptation to believe the lies that the enemy tries to use to overtake our minds. These lies are introduced to us to bring fear and cause us to doubt what we've heard and received from God. Fear is not from God and is in fact the enemy of faith. It is used to move us from the place of confidence in Christ to doing things on our own, without the benefits of Christ as our source.

2 Timothy 1:7King (KJV) [7] For God hath not given us the spirit of fear; but of power, and of love, and of a sound mind.

God doesn't respond to fear and the enemy knows this. He knows that God is moved by our faith in Him. When we lose faith, we also lose our connection to divine power. Just as faith is the key to opening up the windows of heaven, fear is the way to shut those same windows.

Sadly, the church has been instrumental in using God's word to teach that God is a punisher for sin, far more than they have shared that He is an expression of perfect love. Though I had spent many years in church, I later discovered I didn't truly know what it meant to have Jesus Christ as Lord and redeemer. This is why I kept trying to redeem myself. The faith I did have was in God's ability to strengthen me to continue working on the never ending list of tasks I had so I wouldn't completely lose my mind. That is not the blessed life God promised us! You can't produce abundant life through your works. It comes from what you believe about God, not from your confidence in your own abilities.

Part of the confusion that Christians face is locked up in not truly knowing the creator of all things. Ultimately, my desperation led me to a deeper relationship with God and that relationship led me to understand Him and His word. Without seeking Him, so many folks stay in confusion and bondage about who He is and what He is actually saying. I professed to have freedom and even shared the scripture that proclaimed "Whom the Son sets free is free indeed," but it is impossible to believe in a truth that you don't even know about.

The message about our righteousness should be a clear one. It is supposed to enhance faith, not increase fear. I spent years never quite sure if I had performed to God's standard or not. I also perpetuated this cycle of spreading fear when I taught assuming that God needed to instill fear in individuals to get them to submit to Him. This is a total contradiction of who He is. I remember once witnessing to someone and I was basically telling her she needed to turn her life around or else. I told her how awful hell was and that she didn't want to go there. I will never forget the look on her face as I spilled out my self-righteous, judgmental statements, presuming I knew what she needed without any consultation or leading from God. Finally, when I was done, she shared that she had no fear of hell because her life was already hell. This was something I had never considered and it made me stop and think. Some people's lives are in such a shamble, our threats about punishment for their lack of what we perceive to be faithful works won't win them. They need a savior, one they can see as a rescuer not a never-to-be satisfied judge. We should be pointing them to the identity of the one who will never fail them and will love them with an eternal perfect love. I believe this is why many people turn away from the church in despair. If you never feel you've obtained the favor you need in God, He is not a viable resource for you, only another source of pain. If we don't have and share with others the true understanding of God's love, mercy and kindness, we are not sharing the good news at all. Love is a much stronger weapon than fear and once people know how much God loves them, it is much easier to convince them He is there to help, not hurt.

1 John 4:18 (KJV) 18 There is no fear in love; but perfect love casteth out fear: because fear hath torment. He that feareth is not made perfect in love.

So many people live a life that is bound by fear. That is why our messages about God must be very clear. This is not something we do by intimidating people into obedience. With enough pressure, you might be able to change what someone does, without changing their mind. God desires our hearts to be submitted, not our actions. Ultimately, He will recognize us not by what we do, but who we are and who we are will change what we do. I must say again that we have to be careful as we share God's message that we don't make God's wrath bigger than His love. Our commission is to witness to the world separating the facts men experience here on earth from the truths God has established in heaven.

Fight the Good Fight

Our belief in Christ gives us the power to do everything He's asked us to do to live a life reflecting His image. Though we don't have to work for our righteousness under the covenant of grace, we do have to maintain our faith. This requires us to continuously build up our faith in God by hearing His word, spending time in His presence and lifting Him up in praise.

We have to be willing to contend for the faith. To contend is to struggle in opposition. You must be willing to wrestle with and overtake bad thoughts to affirm that what you believe is true.

Jude 1:3 (KJV) [3] Beloved, when I gave all diligence to write unto you of the common salvation, it was needful for me to write unto you, and exhort you that ye should earnestly contend for the faith which was once delivered unto the saints.

You must be careful to keep the mind of Christ and reject anything that will cause you to lose your faith.

2 Corinthians 10:5 (KJV) [5] Casting down imaginations, and every high thing that exalteth itself against the knowledge of God,

and bringing into captivity every thought to the obedience of Christ;

Paul said it best when he spoke to the Corinthians in the second chapter of Corinthians.

Corinthians 2:2 (KJV) ²For I determined not to know anything among you, save Jesus Christ, and him crucified.

If you are acquainted with the Apostle Paul's story in the bible, it is one that should build our faith in the fact that even the worst individuals can be transformed. Paul had misguidedly persecuted Christians until he had an encounter with Christ and his mind was transformed. Once he received the knowledge of Christ by faith, he was careful not to mix it with other knowledge. He traded his ideas for the mind of Christ.

The bible proclaims that we are in this world, but not of it. This means that we physically operate and experience the limitations of this world, but our hearts are rooted in heavenly places where there are no limitations. Still we are surrounded by the world's influences. We have to continue to transform and renew our minds in Christ to assure that we keep the faith that is required to tap into the supernatural. If we choose to lean on our own understanding and do not maintain our faith, we can be pulled into doubt and self-righteousness. It is a daily commitment and one I did not practice as I should have. This is how I found myself in the middle of a season in my life where I felt like giving up, even though I was walking with God. In truth, I was sometimes walking ahead of Him and at other times not walking at all.

Please be assured, our faith will be tested by what may seem to be the most impossible situations, and still, we will have to have faith in God. *The foundation for every act of disobedience is our failure to believe God above our situations.* If we don't believe Him, we won't obey Him. Continuing to do things our way rather than God's way is sin. The wages of a sinful life is death. On the contrary, those who receive Christ receive every blessing.

The evidence of God we receive through the Spirit of God comes from allowing the Holy Spirit to translate the word into truths our hearts can receive. Once received, we have the ability to see impossible things coming to pass so clearly that it is as if there is already tangible evidence of their existence. That is faith!

You don't have to work to be righteous. The blood of Jesus made you righteous, but you do have to wage war to assure that you don't go back to your old beliefs. This fight is one that is not fought in the physical realm where we experience things with our senses.

Ephesians 6:12-16 (KJV) [12] **For we wrestle not against flesh and blood, but against principalities, against powers, against the rulers of the darkness of this world, against spiritual wickedness in high places.** [13] **Wherefore take unto you the whole armour of God, that ye may be able to withstand in the evil day, and having done all, to stand.** [14] **Stand therefore, having your loins girt about with truth, and having on the breastplate of righteousness;** [15] **And your feet shod with the preparation of the gospel of peace;** [16] **Above all, taking the shield of faith, wherewith ye shall be able to quench all the fiery darts of the wicked.**

So much of the discord I had seen in churches over the years came from a misunderstanding of this principle. We are not to fight each other but the devil that brings with him the spirit of confusion. It is virtually impossible for a group of folks who are walking in faith, putting heavenly things first, fully surrendered to God, to also walk in discord. Confusion comes when we begin to yield to and put our faith in other ideas instead of Gods.

This battle over the control of the mind is one you must wage daily. Thankfully, you are not fighting it alone. You have a distinct advantage over the forces of darkness that have come to cause you to doubt and fear the truths you have received. You have the Holy Spirit to act as your guide. He leads us to truths that override what we experience with our senses and constantly reminds us of what we've heard about God instead of what the devil is trying to tell us. When faced with the world's challenges, there are times we have to really reinforce our truths. This isn't always simple, but through Christ, it is always possible.

You have to be aware that the devil is like a commercial that plays over and over again telling you that you lack something. No matter how much you have or how good you are, he will always try to put you in a state of discontentment so that you will seek wholeness from sources other than God. This is what happened in the Garden of Eden. Adam and Eve went from trusting and believing in God as their father and the source of everything, to somehow believing He had withheld something from them. They were convinced that they lacked something and had not truly been given everything they needed or wanted. The adversary wants us to believe that God isn't able to really be our provider or even worse that we can provide for ourselves.

143

Genesis 2:8-9 (KJV) [8] And the LORD God planted a garden eastward in Eden; and there he put the man whom he had formed. [9] And out of the ground made the LORD God to grow every tree that is pleasant to the sight, and good for food; the tree of life also in the midst of the garden, and the tree of knowledge of good and evil.

Genesis 2:15-17 (KJV) [15] And the LORD God took the man, and put him into the garden of Eden to dress it and to keep it. [16] And the LORD God commanded the man, saying, Of every tree of the garden thou mayest freely eat: [17] But of the tree of the knowledge of good and evil, thou shalt not eat of it: for in the day that thou eatest thereof thou shalt surely die.

Genesis 3:1-5 (KJV) Now the serpent was more subtil than any beast of the field which the LORD God had made. And he said unto the woman, Yea, hath God said, Ye shall not eat of every tree of the garden? [2] And the woman said unto the serpent, We may eat of the fruit of the trees of the garden: [3] But of the fruit of the tree which is in the midst of the garden, God hath said, Ye shall not eat of it, neither shall ye touch it, lest ye die. [4] And the serpent said unto the woman, Ye shall not surely die:[5] For God doth know that in the day ye eat thereof, then your eyes shall be opened, and ye shall be as gods, knowing good and evil.

Though God had given Adam and Eve abundant life in the garden, just the idea that there was something more they did not have moved them from a life of rest and access to everything by faith to lives filled with labor and toil. This is the same battle man faces today. We must learn to use the word of God as our sword and faith as our shield to ward off the lies and deceit of the devil.

I remember when my kids were little; they would sometimes watch cartoons on Saturday mornings. Our cabinets were filled with the latest kid cereals. There were also items in the refrigerator that could have easily been prepared for a meal. I recall that the commercials that came on during the Saturday morning cartoons advertised primarily two things, toys and fast food. They marketed these products to kids when they knew they would be watching. My kids would get up from the TV sometimes and run to find me so that they could request a certain kind of meal or toy. I can remember them hollering, "I want a happy meal." I would often respond, "You'd better be happy you have a meal!" Whatever I had in the kitchen was more than enough for them, but they had been convinced by what they saw that they needed more. Isn't this the same principle we operate in when we put our faith in things to satisfy our flesh; gathering up stuff we can't afford? So much of the strife in our world today is caused by buying things we think we need to make us happy, then stressing about how we'll pay for them. Faith should never be in what you possess, like any false idol, objects are powerless to save us.

I remember one Christmas my daughter wanted this dog. I think it looked like a Dalmatian. It was the latest electronic toy and not easy to get. You had to go online to program it so that it would respond to human commands much like a real dog. It was a really popular toy that Christmas and I can't tell you what a sacrifice it was to get that dog. She was overjoyed when she opened it and when she finally got it to work, it barked and barked and drove everyone crazy, including her! Finally, late into the night on Christmas, that dog was still barking. She turned that dog off and put it up and I don't ever remember her playing with it again, but she "had to have it!"

The devil doesn't have any new tricks in his bag, but uses the same temptations today that he used in the garden. He will tell us, "God doesn't really mean what He says. There are other sources for what you want. You don't have to depend on Him." We battle his temptations by resisting them. The ability to resist is wrapped up in who we trust. If we want to believe truth, remember, we have to follow the Holy Spirit.

John 14:26 (KJV) ²⁶ **But the Comforter, which is the Holy Ghost, whom the Father will send in my name, he shall teach you all things, and bring all things to your remembrance, whatsoever I have said unto you.**

The Spirit speaks with knowledge of not only what we see in the natural, but what is possible in the supernatural. It is our connection to the mind of Christ and therefore our connection to heaven on earth. The challenge is to continue to strengthen your faith, always listening intently to the Holy Ghost so that no matter what you face, you will be victorious and not fall into fear or hopelessness.

It is so vital that we remember that faith is believing even when there are not visible signs of what we are believing for. In fact, faith often requires us to defy all of our senses. We may not be able to experience the things we have received by faith as we typically would experience the world around us. Christians are called to believe not only in things that appear to be impossible, but we must also believe in things that may not immediately produce tangible evidence. This alone is a test of the measure of faith we have. Most of us have been taught that proof is something we experience through our senses. So what do you do when you don't see any evidence in the natural realm, but you know for sure you have experienced it during your time with God in the supernatural? You have seen the end of your situation as clearly as if you received the outcome already. This is how people of faith are able to thank God in advance. By faith, they have already received the things they are asking for. Believing that we will receive, however, is only the beginning, we must keep hearing the word of truth to continue to believe what God promised.

During my times of greatest difficulty, there was a battle going on in my mind. My challenge, even after I began to dive into the word of God, was with what I believed; whose voice I chose to hear. This constant struggle for control of what we put our faith in requires us to fight a continuous battle over our mind to ensure that we don't move from faith to fear or doubt.

2 Cor 10:4-5 (KJV) **⁴(For the weapons of our warfare are not carnal, but mighty through God to the pulling down of strong holds;)** **⁵Casting down imaginations, and every high thing that exalteth itself against the knowledge of God, and bringing into captivity every thought to the obedience of Christ;**

Ephesians 6:10-17 (KJV) **¹⁰Finally, my brethren, be strong in the Lord, and in the power of his might.** **¹¹Put on the whole armour**

of God, that ye may be able to stand against the wiles of the devil. [12] For we wrestle not against flesh and blood, but against principalities, against powers, against the rulers of the darkness of this world, against spiritual wickedness in high places. [13] Wherefore take unto you the whole armor of God, that ye may be able to withstand in the evil day, and having done all, to stand. [14] Stand therefore, having your loins girt about with truth, and having on the breastplate of righteousness; [15] And your feet shod with the preparation of the gospel of peace; [16] Above all, taking the shield of faith, wherewith ye shall be able to quench all the fiery darts of the wicked. [17] And take the helmet of salvation, and the sword of the Spirit, which is the word of God:

When we have faith in the liberty we have in Christ we can be confident our battles are already won. Once we stop believing in Him and take matters into our own hands, we are ill equipped to fight. We must be armed with the weapons God has given us to maintain our position of power over the enemy.

I was able to quote these scriptures from memory. Almost every day I put on the full armor of God, but because I was confusing the covenant of grace by faith with the law, I never experienced the full benefit of this weaponry. Too often, I left my place of faith and attempted to fight my own battles. I didn't understand that my works kept me too busy to actually take the time to dive into God's word and spend time with Him. The more you hear Word, the more faith you have. The more faith you have, the more you experience God's rest and peace. Rest is a sign of absolute trust. When we rest, God works on our behalf.

Though faith is the result of our connection to Christ, we have to keep hearing the word of God to maintain it. We cannot allow ourselves to be part of conversations or situations that are contrary to what God has told us or our faith will be weakened. People who spend too much time talking about their problems instead of their God begin to believe what their problems are saying rather than what God has already said. It is impossible to know and believe the word unless you are constantly taking in the word. In both the physical and spiritual, you are what you eat. Just as food is required every day to keep the physical body strong, so is feasting on the word of God to maintain and strengthen your faith walk.

Romans 10:17 KJV So then faith cometh by hearing, and hearing by the word of God.

Romans 10:13-14 KJV[13] For whosoever shall call upon the name of the Lord shall be saved. [14] How then shall they call on him in

whom they have not believed? and how shall they believe in him of whom they have not heard?

When we invited Christ to be the Lord of our lives, the unction to do so came from something we experienced that gave us the faith to choose Him as our savior. You may not even recognize it as audible words, but an overwhelming feeling that communicated God's love. Maybe it was a feeling you experienced as songs or prayer or the word of God went forth. Somehow God's Spirit communicated with your spirit and gave you the faith to believe God and to receive Him.

God's word is described in the bible as a seed that when planted in your heart, produces a harvest.

Mark 4:20 (KJV) ²⁰ And these are they which are sown on good ground; such as hear the word, and receive it, and bring forth fruit, some thirtyfold, some sixty, and some an hundred.

Like any seed that is planted in the ground, the evidence might not be immediately apparent. There is a lot that goes on beneath the soil that can't be seen right away. In spite of this, you can't stop believing or you'll begin to labor without God instead of resting and you will never see the harvest. When your efforts in ministry or life in general diminish your faith and take you away

151

from God's rest, you are too busy. You have to spend time with God and in His word.

As my relationship with God became more intimate, my faith increased. I began to seek out opportunities to spend time with Him rather than seeing our times together as a burden. I started to talk to Him throughout the day as you would a trusted friend, sharing with Him even the smallest details of my day. These constant conversations made me more aware of His presence. Often during prayer, a scripture would come to mind and I would feel the urging to research its meaning. Even the words in the bible were filled with more richness now that I could envision the one who I was communing with speaking them into my heart. The more I believed, the more my ears were open to hear; the more my ears were open to hear, the more faith I had in God.

I remember the year I was having what I felt was a monumental birthday. I decided that if I didn't want to feel old, I needed to really start working out. The first day I arose with great drive. I was determined to reach my goal. I woke up like this for several mornings; pushing away my fatigue and knowing that if I really wanted to be in good health, I would have to get more disciplined and maintain a daily routine of fitness and a better diet. After the first week or so, there were mornings I felt like I had gravel in my eyes, especially after nights that I didn't get nearly enough sleep. I wanted to abandon my routine on those days, but I knew I would never reach my goal if I did. By my birthday, I was in the best shape I had been in in years. I felt great and had more energy and confidence than I had had in a long time.

To maintaining your faith, you have to do the same thing in the spiritual as you do in the natural. It is a commitment to a lifestyle that requires daily maintenance. Your body is a gift from the creator fashioned with everything you need to survive on this earth. Like food and exercise you take in to sustain our physical wellbeing, faith in Christ is needed to live the abundant life God made available to us. Both require daily activity, and that we are careful about what we consume.

Galatians 2:20 (KJV) [20] I am crucified with Christ: nevertheless I live; yet not I, but Christ liveth in me: and the life which I now live in the flesh I live by the faith of the Son of God, who loved me, and gave himself for me.

Receiving salvation will not stop the constant efforts of our adversary. In fact, we become more aware of his devices, but this is our assurance we will not be caught unaware of his schemes to try our faith. These trials increase our faith.

James 1:2-3 (KJV) ²My brethren, count it all joy when ye fall into divers temptations; ³Knowing this, that the trying of your faith worketh patience.

Our adversary will constantly try to convince us that God is not truly the God of endless possibilities. To choose reliance on ourselves instead of God is to place ourselves under the old covenant of the law of sin. If we remain in a place of sin, we become subject to the consequences of it. Instead we have to follow the leading of Jesus, our master. We are like sheep that must follow a guide to find the best pastures. Faith opens our ears to hear what our master is telling us and to reject what our world is telling us.

John 10:3-5 (KJV) ³To him the porter openeth; and the sheep hear his voice: and he calleth his own sheep by name, and leadeth them out. ⁴And when he putteth forth his own sheep, he goeth before them, and the sheep follow him: for they know his voice. ⁵And a stranger will they not follow, but will flee from him: for they know not the voice of strangers.

Following Christ's requires us to obey Him. If He says, "come on, go this way," our trust in Him moves us in that direction. This act of obedience is the result of faith. It is not produced from the Ten

Commandments; a book of stone tablets that are powerless to change us.

Hebrews 8:7-10 (KJV) **[7] For if that first covenant had been faultless, then should no place have been sought for the second. [8] For finding fault with them, he saith, Behold, the days come, saith the Lord, when I will make a new covenant with the house of Israel and with the house of Judah: [9] Not according to the covenant that I made with their fathers in the day when I took them by the hand to lead them out of the land of Egypt; because they continued not in my covenant, and I regarded them not, saith the Lord. [10] For this is the covenant that I will make with the house of Israel after those days, saith the Lord; I will put my laws into their mind, and write them in their hearts: and I will be to them a God, and they shall be to me a people:**

These tablets without faith merely showed us how wrong we were, but couldn't make us right. Christ leads us to every entitlement we have obtained by grace. Hearing and obeying the Holy Spirit is our assurance that we maintain and enhance our faith and recognize every supernatural opportunity that has been given to us. The mature Christian knows that we are not blessed by our works. Instead, when we trust and rely on Him we will do what He says. Obedience to God equates to discovery of abilities and blessings we could never have uncovered on our own.

I cannot stress enough that faith is the key that unlocks the door to the life you have been asking God for. The Bible is filled with miraculous accounts of people whose lives were forever changed because of their faith in Jesus as the answer to their problem.

Though Abraham and his wife who was barren were old and long past childbearing years, he not only became a father, but was made the father of many nations because he believed God's promises. A woman who had suffered with an issue with bleeding for seven long years was healed because she believed if she only touched Jesus garment that would be enough to heal her. Jairus, the synagogue leader believed Jesus could heal his ailing daughter and even though he received the news she had died, because of his great faith, she was raised to life.

The story of Jairus is one of my favorite stories in the bible because each time I hear it I feel strengthened and encouraged. Jairus has just been told not to trouble Jesus because his daughter has passed away. Jesus responds with a simple statement, but it is a phrase that to me is one of the most powerful statements recorded in the bible. This is likely because it is one I have heard

Jesus repeat to me on several occasions as I face life's challenges. The statement is recorded in Mark 5:36 and Jesus tells Jairus, "Don't be afraid, just believe!"

That kind of faith is worth fighting for! So many times I've been tempted to give into worry or doubt and as I turn to Jesus for guidance instead of a long list of thou shalt nots, He simply whispers "don't be afraid, just believe." My Spirit reaches for those words like a thirsty man who finds water. In an instant, without even fully knowing what the solution to my problem will be, I know that it will be wrapped up in my God who is well able to do *exceedingly and abundantly above all that I ask or think according to His glorious riches in Christ Jesus.*

We must surround ourselves with constant affirmation that God's word is true. We have to have a ready response to the ideas and situations the devil will throw at us to make us believe our God is not capable of doing what He's promised. Because the God who lives in us is capable, so are we. Faith makes all things possible. It allows us to experience the world around us, but not be subject to it as long as we continue to fight the good fight of faith.

It is a fight we wage not just for the betterment of our own existence, but to help others see the splendor and power of our

God. There were occasions where I felt the nudging of the Spirit to speak to someone, but I lacked the confidence. As my faith increased, so did my assurance in Him. Once you are certain of who you are in Christ and have experienced the fruits of leaning on Him as your only source, you must do all that you can to maintain trust in Him.

Hebrews 10:35 (KJV) Cast not away therefore your confidence, which hath great recompense of reward.

The Works of Faith

I am a very sensitive person. I cry at the funerals of people I barely know and share the joy of folks reuniting in airports that I have never seen before and likely will never see again. I am mildly amused at the empathy I have for people, and at the same time, consider it part of my call to serve others. It is a gift as long as I allow God to temper it and not let the devil take advantage of it. As I began to receive God's restoration, this empathy, coupled with my newfound faith in God gave me the ability to reach out to others to share His love in a way I never had before.

One day I went for blood work at a lab. As I was sitting and waiting for my turn, I saw a woman approach the lab in a motorized wheel chair. She struggled for a few minutes with the door and came in. She looked as if she were not well cared for and appeared to be on her own and doing her best. After watching her for several minutes at the reception desk, it was clear that she only had limited use of her hands and no use of anything below the waist. It's not that I have never seen anyone in this condition before, but this particular day I felt a tugging on my heart to do something to help this woman. I continued to sit in the chair wrestling with what I knew was an urging from God to intervene in some way. The waiting room was packed and I didn't want to appear odd or out of line in approaching this woman so I just sat there. When my name was called, I felt a sense of relief and walked right past her and into the room to have my blood drawn. I thought I had escaped God's nudging, but it became even more intense. I was having a conversation with God and trying to convince Him that I didn't know what to do. The truth was I didn't want to do anything. Finally I got a leading to simply touch this woman and bless her. I got up from the chair and as I exited, I made a point to walk over to her in front of all those people. Now the room had even more people than before, but I knew I had to obey. I felt my face getting flushed as I gently laid my hand on hers and said, "God bless you." She was clearly moved by the gesture and so was I. Somehow I knew I had just delivered something supernatural to that woman. It is possible that she could have received the manifestation of healing without my intervention. I am not even sure that the Holy Spirit's guidance was for her, though she appeared to brighten up once I released the words. If not for anyone else, the act of obedience by faith I had just performed was for me. I wanted something to happen to relieve that poor woman's suffering. I desperately wanted her to be better. It is as if God knew my heart and shared, "you can help her if only you can believe!" Ultimately, though it took some coaxing, my desire to help her and to obey God outweighed my fear of what others would think. I never saw it, but I believe that God did the impossible on her behalf and brought healing to her body.

God was teaching me that my faith was powerful enough to move mountains in not only my life, but the lives of others. In Matthew the 17th chapter, Christ's disciples are faced with a boy who is demon possessed. They are unable to heal him so he is brought to Jesus who promptly drives the demons out. The disciples are curious as to why they were not able to do what Jesus did and He shares that it is their lack of faith.

Matthew 17:20 (KJV) ²⁰ And Jesus said unto them, Because of your unbelief: for verily I say unto you, If ye have faith as a grain of mustard seed, ye shall say unto this mountain, Remove

hence to yonder place; and it shall remove; and nothing shall be impossible unto you.

Have you ever seen a mustard seed? It is so tiny you can barely hold one in your hand. Our faith is powerful! What does your faith accomplish when it's bigger than a mustard seed if a mustard seed can move a mountain?

The love of God in me moved me to want to help that woman, but I had to rely on my belief that Christ, the healer living inside of me had empowered me to administer that healing power. God's word is clear; Christ bore our sickness and disease on the cross. If He already bore it, the devil doesn't have the right to make us bare it again, but if he can convince us that this isn't true, we will suffer affliction. We may experience sickness while on this earth, but we have to hold fast to the truths God delivered in the world about our healer, Jesus Christ. I was, that day in the lab, only a distribution center for what God had already made available to that woman on the cross. I didn't see it in the physical, but my faith activated the manifestation of what God had already made available to bless her life.

Hebrews 11:1-3 (KJV) Now faith is the substance of things hoped for, the evidence of things not seen. ² For by it the elders

obtained a good report. [3] Through faith we understand that the worlds were framed by the word of God, so that things which are seen were not made of things which do appear.

We must continue to tell ourselves that even if we don't see the supernatural realm with our human eyes, it is still real.   I once heard my pastor say that a fact may not be what is true. He went on to share that it is a fact that you can't part a sea, and yet Moses did it. It is a fact that you can't raise folks from the dead, and yet Jesus did it. The truth is all of the signs and wonders that Christ performed were impossible things for man to do. Even His birth defied our logic. It is a fact that conception of a human takes a male and a female and yet the truth is God did it by the creative power of His Spirit. The creator of heaven and earth and all things therein goes beyond our small reasoning. This is why it is abundantly important that we listen to the Spirit of Truth, the Holy Spirit. It will share with us what is true in the midst of our facts and if we can believe it, we will see it. Don't forget that by faith we will often see it first in our Spirit as it bears witness with God's Spirit, but eventually, it will manifest itself if we can only believe.

Our world has turned good and evil into a miniseries to be played out on movie and television screens and in books. This has desensitized so many people into believing that the supernatural isn't real. Still, we know through the Holy Spirt that it is more real than what we see. In fact, the things we see are only temporary. What God has established is all that is lasting.

2 Corinthians 4:18 (KJV) [18] While we look not at the things which are seen, but at the things which are not seen: for the things which are seen are temporal; but the things which are not seen are eternal.

Once we are walking in God's righteousness, we need only believe. Our belief is in the new covenant we received because Christ became our sacrifice. This covenant is not as rigid as the law because it doesn't have to be. Instead of asking man to walk according to the old laws, which God knew He could not do, He sent Christ to perfect what the law required for sin which was a perfect sacrifice. Our job is to believe it has been done. The laws are written in us, not on stones, but on our hearts which now serve as our spiritual compasses.

We serve a glorious father that devised a plan to assure that we could eternally be righteous in His eyes. So much of what I had become, was based on my need to be righteous. I never felt worthy enough for God's best. This is the beauty of grace, it justifies you and you no longer have to work to justify yourself. Jesus did the work, we have to receive it and walk in it. Finally, I believed that the laws that the Spirit of God had written on my heart included a declaration to the world that I was now and forever, more than enough. When God saw me He saw me through the blood of Christ and therefore redeemed from the consequence of sin. I was now a reflection of Him.

Romans 5:17 (KJV) [17] For if by one man's offence death reigned by one; much more they which receive abundance of grace and of the gift of righteousness shall reign in life by one, Jesus Christ.)

Romans 3:19-26 (KJV) [19] Now we know that what things soever the law saith, it saith to them who are under the law: that every mouth may be stopped, and all the world may become guilty before God. [20] Therefore by the deeds of the law there shall no flesh be justified in his sight: for by the law is the knowledge of sin. [21] But now the righteousness of God without the law is manifested, being witnessed by the law and the prophets; [22] Even the righteousness of God which is by faith of Jesus Christ unto all and upon all them that believe: for there is no difference: [23] For all have sinned, and come short of the glory of God; [24] Being justified freely by his grace through the

redemption that is in Christ Jesus: [25] Whom God hath set forth to be a propitiation through faith in his blood, to declare his righteousness for the remission of sins that are past, through the forbearance of God; [26] To declare, I say, at this time his righteousness: that he might be just, and the justifier of him which believeth in Jesus.

Romans 10:4 (KJV) [4] For Christ is the end of the law for righteousness to everyone that believeth.

2Corinthians 5:21 (KJV) [21] For he hath made him to be sin for us, who knew no sin; that we might be made the righteousness of God in him.

There is a wonderful circle that is perpetuated by the love relationship we have with God through Christ. This relationship makes us hungry for prayer and conversation with God. The revelation I get during communion with God makes me more desirous of His word. The more word I get the more understanding I get. The more understanding I get, the more faith I get. The more faith I get, the more manifestation I see on the earth. This manifestation is not just for me, though I benefit greatly from God's favor being on my life. I also benefit from walking in obedience because I now trust and believe in what He has entitled me to do as well as what He is asking me to be. The tangible evidence, the substance of what God has given me is also for those who do not believe yet. It is a sign to those who do not have the ability to see in the Spirit that God is real. When the unexplainable, the supernatural, the miraculous happens as a result of our faith it is a sign and wonder for someone else. We receive the benefits, others bear witness of it, and God gets the glory!

CHAPTER 6

I'VE GOT THE POWER

The minute my daughter had her driver's permit she wanted to drive. Teaching her to drive was one of the most frightening things I have ever done. Her driving scared both her little brother and I. I remember each time the car came to a stop, he would scream at me from the back seat to let him out. While she did have some driving ability, it became quickly apparent that she needed a considerable amount of practice to actually be able to drive. She was so eager to experience the independence that a car would bring that she was a lot more willing to drive than she was able. I was concerned because her presumption that she was already skilled enough to drive kept her from being as attentive as I wanted her to be to the requirements of safe driving. I remember on one occasion, in spite of my repeated attempts to get her to stop the car at a stop sign, she continued to slowly drive past it,

169

pausing only briefly. While she disregarded my instructions, I watched in horror as we headed toward oncoming traffic, and then I finally lost it. If you've ever taught a headstrong teenager how to drive, it's likely you can relate to my experience. My daughter's desire to drive far outweighed her judgement on the road. She focused on the outcome, not the wisdom it would take to achieve it.

It didn't help that we had already purchased the car for her and she could see it parked in our driveway. After our initial lessons, I decided, though the car was hers, that until she could show me she had mastered the skill of safe driving, she would not receive it. No good parent, who loves their child, will knowingly place them in a position of harm or danger. Had I done this, the car would have been a curse, not the blessing we intended it to be.

If you read the bible, there is no question about the fact that God has blessed His children. We are already blessed, Deuteronomy declares; "in the city and field, coming in and going out." This blessing is an empowerment to prosper. It is the ability that is poured out on us because of God's favor upon our lives. This gift will not just assist us in obtaining things, but in demonstrating the characteristics of Christ.

It would have done my daughter no good to take possession of a car that she wasn't mature enough to drive. There was no question about the fact that it was her car, but she was still stuck getting rides from other folks until she was mature enough to follow my instructions about the safe use of the car.

God desires the same things for us. He has, His word declares, given us access to every good thing, but receiving these things requires a level of wisdom and maturity.

Galatians 4:1-7 (KJV) Now I say, that the heir, as long as he is a child, differeth nothing from a servant, though he be lord of all; ² But is under tutors and governors until the time appointed of the father. ³ Even so we, when we were children, were in bondage under the elements of the world: ⁴ But when the fullness of the time was come, God sent forth his Son, made of a woman, made under the law, ⁵ To redeem them that were under the law, that we might receive the adoption of sons. ⁶ And because ye are sons, God hath sent forth the Spirit of his Son into your hearts, crying, Abba, Father. ⁷ Wherefore thou art no more a servant, but a son; and if a son, then an heir of God through Christ.

When we were sure she was ready, we gave our daughter the car and she no longer had to rely on other people to drive her. We made provisions for her to have what she desired, but did not allow her access until she demonstrated the ability that was consistent with the responsibility.

The Word is Power

What we obtain through the word of God is powerful. Like my instructions to my daughter, the bible is our instruction manual. It is not intended to be a deterrent from the lives of abundance so many of us long for. Its purpose, in fact, is to reveal to us the power we've received through Christ to have more than enough. So many people see the bible as a book of rules; obstacles to having fun or enjoying life. This is a clear sign that they don't really understand the content of the bible. The bible is a roadmap to supernatural empowerment through Christ. It provides the ability to go beyond the mediocre lives so many folks are living.

Eventually, when my daughter yielded to my instructions, though she was still a little shaky in her driving skills, we allowed her to start driving on a limited basis. She ultimately became a good driver, but still, to my horror, I actually discovered much later, that the car was in worse shape than I had imagined. She shared with me that each time she pressed the brakes, her little brother, who was her constant nemesis and usual passenger, would fly into the back seat. His seat clearly was not bolted in properly, a situation we could have easily remedied if she had let us know. My suspicion is that she did not share with us her brother's plight because it gave her great joy to see him fly into the backseat at every stop or quick turn. She may have been a better driver, but she clearly hadn't matured in other areas!

There is no question that God loves us, but that love will not allow Him to make things available to us that we are not mature enough to have. Maturity comes as our minds are transformed. This transformation takes place when we listen and meditate on what God has said rather than what our world declares. Constantly renewing our thoughts is our guarantee that our lives will be a demonstration of the Christ that lives in us. We can be saved by grace, but not fully receive the entitlements that grace allows because our minds have not been transformed.

Romans 12:2 (KJV) [2] And be not conformed to this world: but be ye transformed by the renewing of your mind, that ye may prove what is that good, and acceptable, and perfect, will of God.

Our transformed or renewed minds activate the power of God in us to do things beyond our natural abilities. In other words, when we think like God and have His eternal vision, our tasks become easier and our minds are fixed on His limitless possibilities, rather than our limitations.

God loves us and wants us to be blessed and experience His goodness in every area of our lives. I didn't really understand this during the years where I labored in hopelessness trying to obtain His blessings. My works didn't manifest God's best; instead I used my power to try and gain access to abilities He had already given me through Christ. We must learn how to both access and utilize God's power effectively; otherwise, though we are entitled to His blessings, we will never experience them. Instead, we will be bound to lives where we continue to be slaves to our own efforts. I knew this type of frustrating, powerless existence all too well. This is why I was able to go back and forth in my walk with God; at times effectively living and teaching, and at other times depressed and feeling defeated. I wanted to find the way to move God to do the things that I felt would lead me to a better life. I didn't understand that God had already given me the power to do those things.

I once heard an illustration that used as an example the pin numbers that we use to access our bank accounts. Our faith, like the pin we use at the bank, is how we access the heavenly account that has been set aside to empower us. This means, our emotional pleas may not grant us access to God, but growing faith by the knowledge of His word will. Can you imagine standing in front of the kiosk at your bank and pleading for the money to just suddenly appear? Its appearance is not based on your desire to have it, but your ability to understand the principles that are needed to obtain access to it. Those who fail to understand the Bible, God's instruction manual, may never fully operate in the power God gave us to rule.

I have seen people in desperation petition God and then become disenchanted and angry with Him because He did not perform for them. God may be touched by our infirmities, but He is moved by our faith. Often, we are asking Him to do what He has already done and we simply need to believe it and obey His instructions to see a change in our circumstances. As long as the devil can continue to keep us thinking like a child, we will never see the abundant life that is the entitlement of every Christian.

Who's Supplying the Power?

Though my life was busy and challenging, it wasn't without moments of happiness. I shared countless wonderful days with my family and friends. I have endless memories of holidays with my six brothers and sisters. Even after we were adults, we would still congregate at my parents' house for the holidays and bring all of our children. It was an instant party and just like when we were kids, because there were so many of us, everyone wanted to be at our house. There was always noise, and chaos, and fun! As my children got older, we too began to create holiday memories. I love to bake and my table looked like something from the food network all holiday season. I started baking in October and didn't stop until I was five pounds heavier, around January. My husband and I made a point of taking our children on vacation and seeing them happy was always the absolute joy of my life. I also sat at more freezing football games, and track meets than I can tell you and I wouldn't trade a minute of it.

Still, with all of this, and all of my accomplishments, there was always an underlying feeling that I was not good enough, not worthy. Over the years, the happy distractions became fewer and fewer and my pain and the feelings of hopelessness more apparent as my life began to fall apart. I had experienced the power of God moving in my life, but I was far more aware of my limitations than I was of God's endless possibilities. I grew more and more tired, not just from the hard work of all my self-efforts, but from working that hard without getting the results I so desperately needed. Our limited power cannot compare with God's limitless capability.

I worked to satisfy an insatiable desire to feel better about myself and the world around me. Though I had wonderful days, mixed in with my joy were far too many emotional lows, and I had years of dealing with recurring bouts of depression.

Some people stop and simply hide when they are dealing with stress, but for me, the solution was in trying to feel better. I don't even think I was fully aware that all those self-efforts were my feeble attempts to control my life. The irony is that the more I tried to control it, the more out of control it became. The inadequate power supply I was connected to back then was me. I relied on my own abilities and talents to do what only God could do in my life. How can you accomplish heavenly tasks using earthy means?

The source of our power will determine the strength of our service. One of my pet peeves is pushing the buttons on the TV remote control and having it only work intermittently. This is a sign that the batteries are going out. I don't know why, but changing the batteries is something I don't like to do, but it gets frustrating when one day the remote works, and the next day it doesn't until it finally goes out altogether. This is what our lives looks like when we work apart from the benefit of the Holy Spirit. You can be in a cycle of working outside of the realm of the supernatural and not even be aware of it, especially if a good amount of your time is spent accomplishing tasks for other people. The praise of others becomes a substitute for pleasing God. We often assume that our works become the evidence for our worth. This is simply not true and eventually, you will come to the end of yourself, or worse, die trying.

Though I did a pretty good job of hiding my discontentment from the world, my children and husband saw all of my efforts. I was preaching a lifestyle to the world that I didn't model for the ones who needed to see it the most. I was always doing something, always busy and usually rushing and frustrated, dragging my poor kids along for the ride. Because I constantly relied on my strengths, I was left powerless to really fight the constant onslaught of the enemy. So much of my efforts were used to help me keep my mind off of all of the issues I should have been facing. I wanted my family to love Jesus, but my life of labor toward obtaining righteousness actually worked against me and I was often in the way of them seeing His goodness.

There were so many sacrifices that were made to give us God's endless supply of power, and it is all for nothing if we don't receive it. Though Jesus gave His life and it was not taken from Him, His suffering and pain unto death was real. All of this was to give us the ability to overcome any obstacle. Knowing this, we should not spend more time thinking about how we will solve all of our problems than we do meditation on the problem solver.

I had not established a good relationship with Jesus. Even though I spent some time in prayer, I didn't know Him very well and certainly not as the person of love I later discovered Him to be. I was able to proficiently teach about the principles of empowerment through Christ, but at times struggled to believe in the power of the words I shared with others. Instead, I spent a good amount of time meditating on my "to do" list when I should have been meditating on the Word of God. I was so preoccupied with making my life better, I thought little of the ability that I had already been given to experience a better life.

When I shared my efforts and struggles with others, it was another way for me to gain their approval and justify the life I was living. The more I received accolades the more I believed my life of defeat was a part of God's plan. People often commented on my strength, and skillful multitasking. I mistakenly thought attributing my strength to God made all of my self-righteous efforts alright. Though the works looked good, the motives were powered by my need for self-actualization, not God glorification. There is little glory for God in our constant conversations about our challenges and how we overcame the obstacles by working until we were tired and grumpy. Functioning in our own power to create opportunities for others to glorify our efforts rather than our God is the wrong motivation. I presumed my conversations about all of my hardships were my testimony. The problem was that at times, I talked more about the challenges than I did about God being the solution. Looking back, my conversation was a reflection of my heart. I questioned whether God would show up and be the solution I desperately longed for. At best, I hoped He would strengthen me to work until I manifested my own solution.

Have you ever made the mistake of asking a certain brother or sister in the church how they are? Not just any brother or sister, because most of us are prone to declare that we're blessed no matter what we're going through. The person I'm referring to is the one who is quick to begin to tell you about all of their problems. They are sick and their kids are on drugs and they are broke, and they have a bunion on their right pinky toe! Everything that can possibly be wrong with a human being is always wrong with them. After a half an hour of telling you all of their problems and literally sucking all of the joy and life out of you, they end with a simple confession, "…but God will provide." Do you for one minute believe that there is any power in what they believe? Have they demonstrated that they have the faith that will produce the provision they've declared God will bring? One of the most prominent expressions of God working in us is His power in our lives. This power is revealed as we put our faith in Christ and not ourselves.

Think on Those Things

Trusting God puts us in a state of rest that allows us to hear and believe God and not our situations. When we receive Christ as our savior and put our trust and faith in Him we receive incredible power. This power, when witnessed by others can be a seed of hope that leads to salvation for them.

John 1:12 (KJV) 12 But as many as received him, to them gave he power to become the sons of God, even to them that believe on his name:

I didn't realize at the time that though I wore my suffering, aches and pains as a badge of honor, it didn't glorify God at all. Our struggles are an opportunity to glorify God, not just as we endure them, but as we receive His power to overcome them. The ability to receive that type of power came as I began to comprehend the measure of God's love for me. Once I had this understanding, it made it easier for me to accept that I was really forgiven. I was not just forgiven, but had been made righteous through Christ and had overwhelming, undeserved favor on my life. Favor entitled me to supernatural abilities to do things beyond the limitations of my human comprehension. Through the wisdom found in the word I began to understand just how powerful I was through Christ who provided the strength.

Once we realize that believing God's wisdom leads us to limitless power, we can understand why our minds are a target for the adversary. Constant transformation of your mind through the word of God is necessary to maintain a healthy Christian life. To stand against the facts that will challenge your beliefs each day, you have to read and meditate on the truths found in the word of God.

Philippians (KJV) 4:8 [8] **Finally, brethren, whatsoever things are true, whatsoever things are honest, whatsoever things are just,**

whatsoever things are pure, whatsoever things are lovely, whatsoever things are of good report; if there be any virtue, and if there be any praise, think on these things.

Proverbs 23:7(KJV) **⁷ For as he thinketh in his heart, so is he:…**

What we spend our time meditating on, ultimately becomes who we are. You might feel God's urging to do something that you would never do based on your personality or perceived ability. These are the very moments when God is trying to demonstrate the strength of His divine authority working through you. He is asking you to activate the truths about Him that you've hidden in your heart and by faith, put them into action.

When our faith is working, it will empower us to follow God's lead and not our own. These acts of obedience provide opportunities for us to discover certain truths about our abilities through Christ. These discoveries increase our faith in the authority we have been given to make impossible things possible. As crazy as some of the things sounded that God asked me to do, my willingness to do them gave me access to resources and experiences I could never have imagined. They also helped me to realize how greatly my witness was impacted by what I believed to be true.

People who do not understand their worth, and as a consequence work all of the time in their own strength, are less effective in demonstrating the goodness of God to others. I thought it was a compliment when people told me they could never do all that I did until I realized what they were really saying is that they wouldn't want to do all that I was doing; it was too much! When you work like this you're not just ineffective because you are tired, but also because often you are rigid, judgmental and impatient. The abundant life we are inviting others to share with Christ is not reflected in our frustrated fatigue. Only through the love of God does faith work. When our weariness compromises our love walk, it also compromises our ability to impact the lives of others.

Galatians 5:6 (KJV) For in Jesus Christ neither circumcision availeth anything, nor uncircumcision; but faith which worketh by love.

This could be why there are so many faithful, dedicated, loyal, mean, hateful, cantankerous church workers! They're doing the work, but they've stopped resting in God's ability and are instead working on their own. The minute we leave God's strength and start operating in the principles of the old covenant – the law that requires us to work; we will also, ultimately stop being a reflection of God's love.

God's love and care is clearly demonstrated when we purpose to live a life that includes regular time in prayer and in the presence of God. Once you leave the confidence of grace, you are likely hearing more of what the enemy is saying than what God is, and you're not spending enough time in His Word and His presence. Remember, faith comes by hearing, and hearing, and hearing.....not having heard. We hear a lot of things each day. Whose voice are you listening to?

Romans 10:17 (KJV) So then faith *cometh* by hearing, and hearing by the word of God.

The bible declares in Matthew 13 that the word of God is a seed that when planted in good ground produces abundant fruit. This good ground is your heart. Your heart is your control center, guiding the rest of the body. When the seed of God's word is hidden in the heart, it produces a harvest. This harvest allows man to bring his emotions, intellect, even his physical body under subjection to the will of God. Suddenly, his life is not his own. Giving up your strength appears to be a place of great weakness and vulnerability. Remember what Paul discovered; when we're weak, that's when God is strong. His strength working through us is the ultimate force that no enemy can withstand.

To ensure we are walking in God's power and not our own, the seed of God's word must constantly be planted within our hearts. We have to allow the Holy Spirit to guard that seed by bringing back to our remembrance the words of truth that we have heard. This is how we maintain our confidence in Christ.

Psalms 119:11 (KJV) [11] Thy word have I hid in mine heart, that I might not sin against thee.

Proverbs 4:23 (KJV) [23] Keep thy heart with all diligence; for out of it are the issues of life.

If we're not careful, we will use our strength to present to the world the image of holiness instead of confidently receiving God's transformative truths toward actually being holy through Christ. I thought, the holier I looked, the more of God's power I demonstrated.

I remember blowing my bill money on clothes, and when people complemented me, I would brag on God's goodness. Then when I couldn't pay my bills, I would declare that I was going through a trial financially, but believing God for a supernatural financial miracle. Of course as I shared my noble confession about my endurance through the storm, I didn't bother to tell anyone my troubles were self-inflicted. You know you can't use the money you should dedicate to God for tithes and offerings to buy expensive bags and shoes that you can't afford and then brag to everyone that God blessed you with good deals! I didn't do that, but what I did was just as pitiful. I used my suffering to exalt and glorify myself. Instead of admitting I was walking in fear and needed to change, I solicited others praise for my *endurance* and continued to live a life of defeat and constant, frustrated labor. There is no power in that and no honor, and worst of all, sometimes, because I was so empty, I was ill equipped to share the power God provided to change our world.

I once heard that when they train show elephants, they start very young when the animals are little. As you can imagine, like any young animal, they are free spirited so a rope is tied around their ankle and attached to a wooden stake in the ground. Over a period of time, they realize that no matter how hard they pull against the rope, it will only allow them to go so far. They are not strong enough to pull the stake from the ground and eventually, they are convinced of the limitations of the rope, not the possibilities of freedom. Even when they grow up, the memory of this experience keeps them bound in the same way. Though they are much larger and stronger and could clearly break free, they have already been conditioned by their past experiences.

Regrettably, this is what the devil attempts to do to us to keep us from operating in the influence we've been given. There are things that we experienced; often things that took place in our lives before we truly received salvation that the devil tries to use to maintain control. Maybe you are haunted by past failures or weaknesses that keep you in fear and doubt. Christ living in us is more powerful than any burdensome thought the devil tries to throw at us to keep us bound.

Remember, the laws that were written on stone tablets? Instead of strengthening us, they focused our consciousness on sin and weakened us. In that state of weakness we were in the perfect state to cry out and receive a savior; a savior who could come and be our strength. We must be willing to turn to him, however as our only source. When we don't yield to the power of Jesus in us, we are just like those who were under the law; constantly thinking about our failures and trying to compensate for them rather than resting in the assurance that Gods got it. Surrendering to Him provides the hope we need to be the world overcomers He declares we are.

1 John 4:4 (KJV) ⁴Ye are of God, little children, and have overcome them: because greater is he that is in you, than he that is in the world.

Glad Expectation

This hope, defined in Hebrews 11:1, is the source of the faith that empowers the visible evidence of God's handiwork in the earth.

Hebrews 11:1 (KJV) Now faith is the substance of things hoped for, the evidence of things not seen.

This includes not only our blessings, healing, and wholeness, but God's work in us to spread the principles of His kingdom throughout the earth.   Because hope is another necessary component to the authority we've received, it is also a target for the enemy. If he can steal our hope, he prevents us from entering into faith and ultimately impacts the manifestation of blessings that come from our faith. This is why we must be open to the Holy Spirit so that He can guard our heart.

The Greek word for hope in the bible is elpis.   The literal translation for this word is glad expectation. When I hear this translation, I'm immediately struck by the word glad. This is an indication to us that when we have hope, we are waiting with confidence that God is able to do whatever He said He would do. There is no victory in a complaining, hopeless, child who constantly begs and pleads with God because he doesn't understand he has been given authority. Because of the gift of grace, we have the power to go to God in prayer believing that He both can and will do what we've asked for according to His will.

Matthew 21:22 (KJV) And all things, whatsoever ye shall ask in prayer, believing, ye shall receive.

Once you truly believe God, you'll find that there is no room for complaining. Glad expectation produces praise and thanksgiving! It also results in a confession that bears witness to God and the world that you are trusting in Him no matter what you're situations bring. This confession prompts God's angels to act on your behalf and it is packed with power, even the power of life and death!

Psalms 103:20 (KJV) [20] Bless the LORD, ye his angels, that excel in strength, that do his commandments, hearkening unto the voice of his word.

Proverbs 18:21 (KJV) Death and life *are* in the power of the tongue: and they that love it shall eat the fruit thereof.

These scriptures tell you a lot about the state of mind grace puts you in. When we have real faith, we can be confident even as we endure, so confident that we have gladness! I often testified about a victory that I didn't really have. I was not glad, nor was I confident. I was leaning on my own skills and abilities rather than really trusting God. When we are so confident in Christ ability that we actually praise Him while we wait for our miracle, this is a true testimony to be evidenced by all men of the glory of our God.

Please don't underestimate the power that grace gives you, as I did. I was too busy looking at my impossible situations instead of focusing on God's promises and listening to the Holy Spirit. In Mark 9:29 Christ Himself declares, that "nothing is impossible to those who believe." Faith gives us access to supernatural strength that makes the unattainable possible. We need to see our impossible situations as an opportunity for God to show us and the world His abundant power. These situations are occasions where God can be magnified and glorified. We think of the exposure we face when everyone is talking about us and counting us out as a failure. In reality, those trials of our faith are often a setup for God to show Himself strong. So you might be talked about. You might be the favorite topic of conversation for some people, but know this, if you can resist the desire to tuck your tail and run, or even worse, start fighting in your own strength and instead believe God, they will see undeniable truths about the God living in you.

In the book of Daniel in the Bible, there is an amazing story of Daniel who was persecuted because of his faith. The other leaders in the Babylonian kingdom were jealous of him, but could not find any fault in him so they attempted to use the thing that gave Daniel his strength, his connection to God. It appears in this story that he is being persecuted for his beliefs as he is thrown into a den of hungry lions. To everyone's amazement, the lions don't eat him. God actually shuts their mouths, protecting Daniel from any harm and what the devil meant as a display of his power, became a setup to demonstrate the power of the Almighty God.

God has a way of closing the mouths of our enemies just like He shut the mouths of the hungry lions for Daniel, but He won't fight as long as we're fighting. Resist the temptation to use your own power and tear people down and instead, speak life.

John 6:63 (KJV) [63] It is the spirit that quickeneth; the flesh profiteth nothing: the words that I speak unto you, they are spirit, and they are life.

The truths the world will see demonstrated in your life may be things they've never seen before. There is great power in God's manifested truth, especially the truth that is a total contradiction to all of man's facts. Like the truth that Mariah lived for me when against all odds and in the midst of her own personal pain, she thought first of others.

The truth is that through Christ, man was restored to the place of power and dominion God intended in the Garden of Eden. The devil may throw every trick he has against you to make you believe this isn't so, but it is. Once Christ paid for our sins, the power of sin was forever lifted and we were returned to our place of authority to rule on the earth.

Genesis 1:26 (KJV) And God said, Let us make man in our image, after our likeness: and let them have dominion over the fish of the sea, and over the fowl of the air, and over the cattle, and over all the earth, and over every creeping thing that creepeth upon the earth.

The dominion God gave us is the power to govern, rule, and subdue the earth. We should always remember our righteousness through Christ is our access to God's authority. Understanding our worth in Christ and His power working through us, gives us the ability to come out from our old ideas and habits and use His creative power. Only when we operate through this power can we establish the heaven on earth He envisioned "in the beginning." We also need to remember that this ability to rule is not enforced through our physical muscle, but His spiritual strength. Our power is in our capacity to call forth those things that are in heaven to the earth with absolute faith that our words carry the weight of God and therefore will bring manifestation.

One of the greatest revelations I received was the revelation that God was so in love with me, He sent Christ to free me from the captivity of sin. With greater revelation about Christ and how His love is demonstrated, I continue to gain more power through Him. I stopped trying to manipulate situations and use all of my talents and training to make things happen and I began to hear the voice of God through the Holy Spirit and to obey. Even the ministry that I was already committed to changed. It was no longer me working on God's behalf, but God working through me to accomplish His will in the earth.

Faith Works

I once held an outreach for kids who needed a blessing in our community. The outreach was an annual event that eventually grew to include hundreds of participants and dozens of social service providers along with our church. We provided backpacks filled with school supplies and ministered to hundreds of families who desperately needed both resources and encouragement. Our partners in the community provided information intended to educate them on opportunities that could enhance their lives while we sought to strengthen their spirits.

During one of the outreach events I organized, we arrived at the church to find the largest group of needy kids I had ever seen. It was clear the number of backpacks we had was far exceeded by those who were waiting in front of the church to receive them. Seeing the crowd, I took a few minutes to quietly pray, "God, you led me to have this event, you know the need of the people who have gathered here, and I know you are going to meet the need."

I have to tell you that I didn't realize it at the time, but this was a sign of the confidence I had received as I finally began to have faith and trust in God. I can remember earlier years where I would have immediately begun to complain and speak about our lack. There was an occasion a few years before when we had run out of supplies for a similar event and I beat myself up. I found a quiet place and instead of offering up confident prayer, I wept in disappointment. I even got offended by some of the suggestions I received to make the event better for the following year because I felt the event was my personal failure. This was clear evidence of where I was in my journey with God. How on earth could I be offended, overly sensitive, and taking comments personally, unless I had taken on the work myself instead of allowing God to work through me?

In contrast, during this outreach, I listened to the voice of the Spirit of God in me that assured me this was God's event and therefore, there must be provision for it already available to me. I didn't have to see it to believe it; I had to believe it to see it. I firmly planted my feet and decided to believe God and not my circumstances.

Before opening the doors allowing our community in, we asked God to bless each one of those backpacks and multiply them. Finally we'd given out everything we had and our large multipurpose room once overflowing with backpacks looked like an empty storehouse. We had to turn some individuals away but asked them to go outside into our parking lot. We still had a carnival atmosphere outside of the church and our guests were encouraged to enjoy the rest of the day with our community partners; gathering information, playing games and enjoying free food. I walked out of the church to find a young woman who was cursing and clearly extremely angry that we had run out of supplies. I thought twice at first about approaching her as she was not at all happy about the long wait she had had only to be turned away empty handed. Finally, I could not endure her bad language at the entrance to the church any longer and I walked right up to her and grabbed her hands. "What's wrong," I asked. She shared that she had picked up her niece and nephew and was trying to do a good thing by bringing them by to get backpacks and school supplies and we had run out. I pulled her inside the church as I told her I desired to pray for her. I then told her that God saw her heart and would provide and that though it was not the outcome she expected, she would still be blessed. I encouraged her not to act as she had been. Sometimes, people just need you to share your faith to empower them to do what is right and hold on till they see their miracle.

As we were talking, I could hear someone calling my name from the end of our church lot. Finally I was able to make out one of the church members waving a backpack at me. One of our community supporters had a brother who just happened to be a minister. When we ran out of supplies with so many folks left to serve, he called him. He just happened to have a warehouse filled with backpacks stuffed with school supplies. He had brought an entire truck filled with them and even went back when we gave these out and picked up more. Of course, you realize, he didn't just happen to have what it took to supply our need, before God ever birthed in my heart to have the event, He put aside provisions for me. I accessed those provisions by faith. Needless to say, the power of faith that day didn't just bless me, it provided for the needs of dozens of members in our community. I also have to believe that it showed that young lady the power of believing God instead of her circumstances.

Now stop for a minute and think about what would have happened if I had not followed the unction of the Holy Spirit and declared God's provision on what appeared to the physical eye to be lack. Imagine what could have occurred if in spite of actually running out of backpacks, I had not again declared to that young woman that God was going to do something to meet the need. I do not for a minute presume that God would not have met the needs somewhere else, but praise God, because of faith, I was able to take part in the miracle. There is power in believing God that goes beyond our human reasoning. Faith gives us access to supernatural power. By our faith, we are able to tap into the Holy Spirit to provide evidence to an unbelieving world that God, His word, His son, His power, they are all real.

The more my faith was tested, the more God proved His word to me. I recognize that none of us like dry places, but these are opportunities for God to reveal the power He's given us. Anything we believe is possible for us to do; we may be prone to do without so much as giving God any glory at all. It is not until some people face something absolutely dire, impossible and urgent that they turn to Christ, surrender, and acknowledge His work as Savior, Lord, Provider and King. I was learning to live in a submitted state allowing the word of God to govern me so that I would have the faith to govern the world He'd sent me to subdue.

Romans 8:11 (KJV) [11] But if the Spirit of him that raised up Jesus from the dead dwell in you, he that raised up Christ from the dead shall also quicken your mortal bodies by his Spirit that dwelleth in you.

I finally understood that the power to change my life and my world was not given to me because of my works, but in spite of them. If this power was great enough to raise Jesus from the dead, surely it was enough to give me the ability I needed. Once my heart was renewed by the word and the Spirit of God, I began recognize my true destiny. I was no longer a worker moving against the force of God, but a worker together with Christ tapped into endless, supernatural power.

Peace at Last

If you've ever lived a life that does not include total peace, you know the value of having peace of mind. There have been moments, I would imagine, in everyone's life where you would have paid any amount of money to experience rest and restoration. Finally getting to a place where I had the confidence to relinquish my burdens for the peace the bible declares, "That surpasses all understanding" was incredibly powerful. When we receive Christ, we don't just receive salvation from the consequences of sin, but the person of Christ comes to live on the inside of us. Everything Christ is, we become. He is no longer just a story stretched out on the pages of a book, but a living being that lives in and through us. All the promises that God gave us are wrapped up in Christ. So living inside of us is the healer, the deliverer, the provider, and the sustainer. Whatever Christ is, as we receive Him, we become. That's power! He doesn't come to improve us, but to actually replace who we are with who He is.

1 John 4:17 (KJV) Herein is our love made perfect, that we may have boldness in the day of judgment: because as he is, so are we in this world.

CHAPTER 7

STRENGTHEN YOUR BROTHER

I remember the night I finally decided to leave my husband and the home I had lived in much of my adult life. I sat there wishing that somehow a last minute miracle could take place, transforming our marriage into the fantasy I had played and replayed in my mind, but I knew deep down this was not going to happen. I was leaving my home for good.

For someone who fought to always be in control, this was a night of great sorrow for me. I was the woman with the plan after all, and the endless "to do" list. I was leaving, but my mind was screaming, "What are you doing? Where are you going?" My feet just seemed to obey, even as my heart broke. It was a sickening feeling that I carried around for many weeks as I struggled to find myself, but I marvel as I look back, at how carefully God carried me through those early days. He was so gentle with my broken heart, I wasn't even aware I was being carried. For me it was as if I was in a trance, simply existing. I can't even say I engaged in meaningful prayer at first. It was more of a tearful cry for strength and guidance, but I thank God He was able to look beyond my pain to the surrender of my heart. My leaving was not an act of anger, but an act of obedience. It was my way of saying that I would not be bound to fear, but to God.

How many situations have you remained in far too long, situations that you got yourself into without God's guidance or permission? There are so many things that were a blur in that season. What I am sure of however, is that Jesus strength was made perfect in my weakness. I am also certain that each day brought new challenges, but also a fresh supply of God's power and wisdom. I learned things about my capabilities through Christ that I would never have discovered had I remained in a situation He was no longer a part of.

That first night, I went to my daughter's one bedroom apartment. A little later, I moved into my own apartment with nothing but the few bags of clothes and items I had taken with me. I had to start all over, not just my life, but creating a home. Once I was settled into my little place, I didn't want to be around anyone. I was just so ashamed of myself and the condition of my life. Though our church was shutting its doors, I had spent so many years with my small church family and they refused to hear my requests for privacy and began showing up at my apartment unannounced. They even showed up one Saturday to assist me with finding furniture for my modest place. I remember that day very well. They arrived early that morning in trucks and ready to scour yard sales with me. I was moved beyond words and though my little place was a far cry from the nice home I had left, their efforts to help me start to build a new home were therapeutic for me. The love they shared with me during that time was my lifeline to God. You can never underestimate the power of even the small things you do for someone else. Even a new Christian has the power to impact someone else's life. My little church family showed me the unconditional love of God during a time of total brokenness, and through that love, became part of His divine plan to put me back together again. They demonstrated the powerful light of God's word in action for me with acts big and small. Even the smallest gestures meant so much to me during that time of darkness. You would be amazed at what just a small amount of light in a dark place can do to help someone find their way. We are, after all, containers for the *light of the world, Jesus.*

There is no way to interject His presence into darkness and not light it up.

Matthew 5:14 (KJV) [14] Ye are the light of the world. A city that is set on an hill cannot be hid.

Never underestimate your ability to act as God's witness to someone in despair. I don't know where I would be today had those simple acts of kindness not been shown to me; each one a light to guide me along the pathway to God's unconditional love.

Wonder Working Power

When we demonstrate the love and kindness of God to others, we magnify Him. I would imagine that in everyone's life, whether they are aware of it or not, there has been a moment when even a small act of kindness transformed a situation and gave much needed strength. It might have been something done for you that wasn't even extraordinary, just a simple gesture in a moment when you needed reassurance that everything would be alright.

I have learned that this type of power is not contained in us apart from the Holy Spirit. This Spirit is packed with the power to change not only our lives but to transform the lives of others.

Luke 24:49 (KJV) And, behold, I send the promise of my Father upon you: but tarry ye in the city of Jerusalem, until ye be endued with power from on high.

The word *power* used here is from the Greek word dunamis. Dunamis power is dynamic, explosive power that gives us miraculous ability. Our birth into Christ by faith is the key to receiving dynamic power. This power comes with purpose.

Acts 1:8 (KJV) [8]But ye shall receive power, after that the Holy Ghost is come upon you: and ye shall be witnesses unto me both in Jerusalem, and in all Judaea, and in Samaria, and unto the uttermost part of the earth.

The Holy Spirit works in us, giving us the ability to do what is absolutely impossible for us to do on our own. God's desire is for us to share our faith and the good news of the Gospel with others.

When people hear the command to "go", many people are afraid that this includes doing things beyond what they believe to be their capabilities or outside of their comfort zone. God has not asked us to do any of His work on our own, but to first be separated from our own thoughts and fears. Once we have received His power, His desire is that we go out and witness to the world. This means that everything you need to fulfill Christ's commandment to go and reach others is in you. I am alive today because of the willingness of others to adhere to this principle. They allowed the Holy Spirit to use them and showed up just in time to help me.

I recall that one such group that was instrumental in helping me through some of my really tough times was Woman's Aglow. This women's ministry consisted of beautiful women that represented a rich, diverse group. It was made up of women from different backgrounds, denominations, races, and ages. These women came together around a common theme; glorifying Jesus and encouraging one another in the spirit of unity. It was the one place that I didn't feel I had to perform. Each month, as I attended these meetings I felt a glimmer of hope. This was one of the few places, in fact, where I did feel encouraged. At one meeting, I was really struggling, though I was a master at hiding my pain by then. A few days before this particular meeting, I had separated from my husband. It was not known to most people because I was both embarrassed at not being able to work out our problems and at the same time, hopeful we would be able to reconcile. I didn't want other folks speaking ill of us when I was trying to speak words of life on our relationship, so I had kept the separation to myself. While my face didn't show the pain, inside I was hurting.

I went to that meeting and while there, I went into the restroom to wash my hands. As I stood in front of the sink, a woman approached me and said, "God told me to tell you that He sees your pain and He has not forgotten you." You might be thinking that the words she spoke were not profound, but to me, it was as if heaven opened up and God Himself spoke them to my grieving heart. Just in case you have presumed she was responding to some outward indication from me and not the Spirit of God, let me assure you I as a master of disguise and had become pretty proficient at masking my pain. The Spirit of God in her reached out that day and touched my despair. I had never been ministered to by a stranger like that. At that point, I knew little of the prophetic workings of God and I was amazed. I was amazed at both her and God. She was so bold and so confident of what she said to me and she had never seen me before in her life! I could not tell you today what that woman looked like, but I will never forget the way her message of hope made me feel. She drew from the dunamis power she possessed and downloaded the gift of hope into me straight from the throne room of God. It was as if God Himself filled that bathroom with His presence and brought strength to me in my time of weakness. This woman's simple act of obedience was, in that moment, a lifeline for me! I would imagine there have been profound moments in your life too, though you may not have been fully aware of them, when someone did or said just the right thing at just the right time.

There were so many times in my life when similar occurrences took place just when I needed them. Though often small, the care and kindness of God's messengers provided me with glimpses of His love for me and gave me enough encouragement to keep pushing until I could be free. If you have ever felt lost, alone and forgotten, you know how powerful it is for someone to simply say, God knows and He cares or even to let you know it will be alright.

We are instruments that contain the ability to spread eternal life. Once the image of Christ is received in us, its reflection saves others just like it set us free! We only have to yield to the power of the Holy Spirit to know when, who, and how to approach with God's life transforming love. Each of us was formed and fashioned with our own unique ability to shine the light of God. That light does not operate based on our emotions, but is activated by our yielding to the Spirit of God; the Christ that lives in us. Receiving His empowerment is not just a requirement for salvation, but a result of being born again. Once Jesus takes up residency in your heart and mind, you have the ability to produce life. This is exactly what the individuals who kept pushing me toward my destiny did for me.

Among those who came and so graciously cared for me were women of God who simply loved on me. Some days it was an unsolicited complement or a hug. Other days it was sharing of the word of God or prayer. Whatever their offering, they continued to cultivate the seed that God had planted in my heart so many years before. Each individual that obeyed the unction of the Holy Spirit provided just enough water and light to keep my fragile heart alive until it was strong enough to beat on its own.

One of the most profound experiences I recall as I look back at how God used others to deliver me, was an evening when I was busy working in my restaurant. At one time, I ran a small mom and pop restaurant and though it was a tough job, it actually was successful for a while. It was during a period that I was feeling so low; the days were long and exhausting, and I'm sure they felt longer because I was unable to find meaning or purpose in them. Each day became more and more of a struggle. Of course my happy mask did a pretty good job of hiding my true feelings of despair from most people. I always had a ready smile and was a kidder. I believe this is how I was able to live so long in so much pain without it being detected by others. Anyway, I was working when I was approached by a powerful woman of God. She was actually the wife of the Pastor of the church I was attending at that time. I, of course, put on my *"I'm saved, sanctified, and filled with the Holy Ghost"* face and waited on her. She ordered and ate, but my cooking was not the reason for her visit. She was on a mission trip from God. She had a special assignment to meet me right where I was that day at the intersection of lonely, and defeated. She began to tell me all about my desperate condition and as bad as my life was, I was still prideful so I resisted her efforts at first. I was completely suspect of her intentions and was in the midst of telling her that "clearly she did not recognize the challenges of running an important restaurant and having the responsibility that I had," when suddenly, she snatched the mask from my face. "You are living in a fantasy. You've let the fantasy be more real to you than God's word. You're unhappy, but you put on that face to protect yourself. God sent me here to tell you He loves you and that He has more for you." Right there, as *important* as I thought I was, in the middle of my restaurant, with customers sitting nearby and my employees in the kitchen, I broke into tears. It was a hard truth, but one I needed to hear if God was to chip away at the walls I put up to protect myself from my true fears and feelings of worthlessness.

I realize the idea of helping others is a foreign one to so many who share the world we live in today. There is so much emphasis placed on being self-reliant and independent. Often people look at receiving help as a sign of weakness and giving help, as a sign of superiority. Also with so much deception and abuse in our society, those who could provide help are sometimes guarded or unwilling for fear they will be taken advantage of.

Still, our commission is clear from God; we are to go and compel them to come in. This is what this dear woman was doing in spite of my initial defensive response. I do not have the words to describe how that divine appointment changed my life. She was confident beyond my resistance and saw past the facade of my life.

Have you ever responded to someone's truths with your short-sided facts? Be careful! They may be a messenger to answer your prayers for abundant life. Don't assume they don't know you or understand what you're going through. Each of us has a unique story that has been part of the process toward God's ability to use us in reaching out to others. If He sent them, and they had the

Holy Ghost boldness to obey God and approach you, they are equipped to deal with you and your messy life!

Christ Was First

If you truly open up your heart to the splendor that is God's word, you will see so many demonstrations of His unconditional love. Can you imagine knowing that your future includes not only a brutal vicious death, but betrayal by those who you have loved so dearly? This is what Jesus faced on His last night wrapped in flesh on the earth. He sat at a table and broke bread with men who would betray Him and deny having known Him. Still love not only allowed Him to share this meal, but to later save their lives. The men who walked with Christ were ordinary men who had been a witness to extraordinary events, but ultimately, before they received supernatural power, their fear outweighed their faith. God is trying to show us that we don't have to be perfect, but we must be willing to surrender, even if that surrender happens over and over again.

The bible tells us that while we were yet in sin, Christ died for us. Our healing and spiritual empowerment is necessary toward having the power to demonstrate God's love to others. His service to man was not contingent on the condition of our hearts, but the condition of His. God knows we are too selfish to think

214

like this on our own, but once the Holy Spirit has taken up residency in us, we become messengers of what we have experienced. Left to our own thoughts, there are a million reasons why we would likely never approach anyone with the word. Thank God we are not left to our own devices. With His help, we can go and share what we have learned about Christ. This is the great commission.

Luke 14:23 (KJV) And the lord said unto the servant, Go out into the highways and hedges, and compel *them* to come in, that my house may be filled.

Matthew 28:18-20 (KJV) [18]And Jesus came and spake unto them saying, All power is given unto me in heaven and in earth. [19] Go ye therefore, and teach all nations, baptizing them in the name of the Father, and of the Son, and of the Holy Ghost: [20] Teaching them to observe all things whatsoever I have commanded you: and, lo, I am with you always, *even* unto the end of the world. Amen.

I had always been conscious of the fact that my life was not my own. I knew I was part of the larger plan of God to reach the world with the news of our redemption through Christ. I only needed to join my willingness to God's ability, to rise beyond the limitations of my old mindset about God and be a true instrument for His use. Once my mind was rejuvenated, I had a more meaningful understanding of what the *good news* was. I had heard of the Great Commission; God's plan for us to go out and spread the gospel; our redemption and rebirth through Christ. Receiving Jesus Christ as Lord instead of just a judge made obedience to this commission possible for me.

Reach Out and Touch

For years I fed the hungry and had several outreach events helping those who needed a blessing in our community. The service I was performing was not wrong, but sometimes, the source of my strength was. You have to frequently; especially as you move out into the highways and hedges, take time with the message and the messenger. In doing this, the reflection the world sees is no longer you, but the Greater One in you. Once you have truly received this richer truth, there is a super on your natural ability that can reach men and supply resources you could never provide on your own. Again, we must realize that our work, apart from Christ only glorifies us, but when God does it through us, He is glorified in it.

So many people struggle with the idea of sharing the good news because they have not fully received it. Once you have, it won't be such a struggle to share it. Call me a fanatic if you want to, but when you have lived an emotional rollercoaster all your life, seeking peace and joy in all the wrong places and are finally free, you want to tell someone about it!

We were created not only for eternal fellowship with God, but to establish His kingdom on the earth. We are equipped through our faith to war with things in the earth that others stumble over. Built into our faith is the power to bring forth miracles in a way that draws people to God. He desires that every aspect of our lives glorify Him. In the same way that God desired to save us, He also desires that none be lost.

When we understand the creative force we now have in faith, this task isn't daunting, but exciting! Once you truly believe it, you have the ability to fulfill God's instructions for you to share the *good news* with others. The same powerful message that sets us free can set others free if we will be faithful to God's instructions in delivering it.

Mark 16:15-18 (KJV) [15] And he said unto them, Go ye into all the world, and preach the gospel to every creature. [16] He that believeth and is baptized shall be saved; but he that believeth not shall be damned. [17] And these signs shall follow them that

believe; In my name shall they cast out devils; they shall speak with new tongues; [18] They shall take up serpents; and if they drink any deadly thing, it shall not hurt them; they shall lay hands on the sick, and they shall recover.

Luke 24:44-49 (KJV) [44] And he said unto them, These are the words which I spake unto you, while I was yet with you, that all things must be fulfilled, which were written in the law of Moses, and in the prophets, and in the psalms, concerning me. [45] Then opened he their understanding, that they might understand the scriptures, [46] And said unto them, Thus it is written, and thus it behooved Christ to suffer, and to rise from the dead the third day: [47] And that repentance and remission of sins should be preached in his name among all nations, beginning at Jerusalem. [48] And ye are witnesses of these things. [49] And, behold, I send the promise of my Father upon you: but tarry ye in the city of Jerusalem, until ye be endued with power from on high.

This power that Christ promised His followers in Luke; the Holy Spirit, was the gift He gave with His departure from the earth to ensure that we are well able to do what we have been called to do. The same Spirit that leads us out of the darkness of sin into God's marvelous light also assists us in leading others out. When you understand how deeply God loves you, it is not difficult to imagine that He would say to those of us who now clearly understand His love, "go get the rest of my children!"

His command is not unlike mine to my daughter when my son was a little boy. Go and make sure He is alright. I taught them to take care of each other and even though they fought constantly, they did take care of each other.

I remember there was this huge kid who lived near our church and he was a terrible bully! He would pick on my son and the other kids in the church when there were no adults around. One day he was messing with my son and my daughter had had enough. She picked up a large jagged piece of wood and began swinging it wildly at him. I heard all of this shouting and screaming and arrived outside to find her trying to knock that kids head off. She was tired of him picking on her brother and that particular day decided it was going to stop! I was horrified. I screamed her name and because I was over the children's ministry, I took the wood from her and explained as any good Christian minister mom would, that we needed to be kind to each other. I was really talking to that kid, but he seemed completely uninterested and I knew as soon as I wasn't around he would try something with some other kid.

Shortly thereafter, I loaded my kids in the car and headed for home. Not long after we got in the car I turned to my daughter and said, "Good job. Never let anyone beat on your brother." Before you accuse me of being a hypocrite, please allow me to explain. I wanted those children to understand that violence in general is not right. I also wanted my child specifically to understand that that very large, mean spirited bully who never fought fair and always picked on her brother and the other kids needed to be dealt with. Maybe not with a big piece of wood, but someone who had the ability to take him on needed to stand up to him and say "stop, no more messing with my brother!"

Our heavenly father has given us the same permission. "Go out into the world and put that bully, the devil in his place and rescue your brothers and sisters from his beatings. Enough is enough! There was a time when you were too small to deal with him," I hear our Heavenly Father saying, "but I have strengthened you and now that you're *strong in the Lord and the power of his might*, you need to go deal with him and bring the rest of our family home."

This is the message Jesus gave to Peter as He shared His last meal with His beloved disciples.

Luke 22:31-32 (KJV) ³¹ **And the Lord said, Simon, Simon, behold, Satan hath desired to have you, that he may sift you as wheat:** ³² **But I have prayed for thee, that thy faith fail not: and when thou art converted, strengthen thy brethren.**

Jesus shares with Peter that He is not only aware of the intentions of the enemy and his imminent failure in the faith, but was confident that the prayer He prayed for him would restore him after he fell into fear. He is so confident of Peter's conversion by faith that he instructs him to do what we all should do once restored; strengthen our brothers.

Out With The Old – In With The New

For some people, total surrender to God means they walk upright and in obedience right away. This was not my story. While my faith was being fortified, I still had times when I acted like the old me, especially when it came to my conversation. It is important that I am honest about my struggles because they were directly related to the effectiveness with which I impacted others.

The bible reveals that life and death are in the power of the tongue. We are no help to people if we try to minister to them one minute and talk about them the next! You might not intend to be unkind, but that may be the outcome. You may still be hurting and fragmented as I was. As restoration came to me, I realized I had to change the habits I had formed. Even though I was doing so much better, I had already created relationships with folks that included behaviors I no longer wanted to be a part of. The problem was that they still did. The girls I had gossiped with still wanted to gossip. The folks I had inappropriately joked with, or complained with still wanted to find me and do those things. I had to separate myself from them. It was uncomfortable, but I was so committed to God, it was not as hard as you might imagine. Ultimately, we cannot be people's unrighteous judge, and minister the gift of salvation at the same time. We can't make them the subject of our jokes and our unkind accusations and speak life upon them. If we truly want to demonstrate that Jesus is our Lord, we have to stop hanging around people and places that keeps us bound to the habits we had under the old lord we served in ignorance. To do this, I had to begin to walk in the principles I was now gleaning from the bible. My old habits of working wouldn't do. If you really try hard, you can change your mind, but only God can change your heart. I wanted to stop seeing only the worst in others who were difficult to love, but it was impossible to do until I first saw myself as Christ saw me.

There is so much power in our words. We have to train our mouths to be instruments of life. You might presume you are powerless to impact the lives of others, but sometimes, even a quiet prayer or bold declaration on their behalf can change it for the better. Jesus once told His disciples, "The Spirit gives life; the flesh doesn't count for anything; the words that I have spoken to you are full of Spirit and life," (John 6:63 NIV).

You need to know that to be used effectively by the Holy Spirit; you don't have to be a bible scholar, but you must be willing to allow the Spirit to be your guide and remind you of the word of God. He will focus you on the love of God and not His judgement. I had to change the way I saw God to change the way I served God. God is a just God, but as important as that, He is also loving. That's why Christ was sent to pay our debts. Any anger God had because of our sin was emptied out on Christ as He endured the brutality of His crucifixion. Every piercing through His flesh produced new possibilities for us as He poured Himself out so that we could receive Him unto ourselves. His sacrifice was our atonement and placed us under a new covenant that no longer requires us to shed our blood, but rather covers our sins in the blood of Christ. Because of this, our sins are not visible to God. In their place is a coat of righteousness that God sees when He looks at us. The challenge is we must see it too. How can God continue to punish you for sins He can no longer see or remember.

Hebrews 8:10-12 (KJV) [10] For this is the covenant that I will make with the house of Israel after those days, saith the Lord; I will put my laws into their mind, and write them in their hearts: and I will be to them a God, and they shall be to me a people: [11] And they shall not teach every man his neighbor, and every man his brother, saying, Know the Lord: for all shall know me, from the least to the greatest.[12] For I will be merciful to their unrighteousness, and their sins and their iniquities will I remember no more.

You must understand God's perspective of our sin so that we have the assurance that He is not like men who never forget our wrongs. This Good News brings the liberty we need to reach others. Once we've received Christ, God not only can't see our sins, but forgets them. If we fall from grace, our sincere change of heart; repentance places us back under the blood. If however, we never believe God unto salvation, we will receive the full measure of God's judgement. So much of what we see in the bible about the consequences of sin is directed at those who do not truly receive Jesus as Lord.

224

John 13:34 (KJV) [34] **A new commandment I give unto you, That ye love one another; as I have loved you, that ye also love one another.**

We have to understand our righteousness in Christ so that we can go and reach others with the confidence that we've been called and justified, and predestined to spread the kingdom of God. The devil will be relentless in his efforts to make us feel unworthy to represent our God. He delights in reminding us of our failures so we have to be careful to stay in contact with Jesus in prayer and yield to the direction of the Holy Spirit.

Man can remember something and bring it up in every argument from the day it happens till he leaves the earth. We have to remember that our God is not like that. Once you receive salvation and the gift of grace, you also receive forgiveness. It is a more powerful gift than you know. This means with God, once we receive Jesus Christ as Lord, we don't received what we deserved, Instead someone else took our punishment and we were given unmerited favor. Grace isn't just our forgiveness; it is the power for us to forgive others. This is important to remember as we consider our charge to impact the world for God.

With restoration came a genuine desire to serve others as Christ wanted. The motivation for my service was no longer a mixture of a desire to serve God and serve myself. When God truly becomes your only source, you do not look to other people or things to supply your needs. This is true liberty!

Receiving Christ is the end of condemnation and the beginning of fruitful service.

Romans 8:1-11 (KJV) There is therefore now no condemnation to them which are in Christ Jesus, who walk not after the flesh, but after the Spirit. ²For the law of the Spirit of life in Christ Jesus hath made me free from the law of sin and death. ³For what the law could not do, in that it was weak through the flesh, God sending his own Son in the likeness of sinful flesh, and for sin, condemned sin in the flesh: ⁴That the righteousness of the law might be fulfilled in us, who walk not after the flesh, but after the Spirit. ⁵For they that are after the flesh do mind the things of the flesh; but they that are after the Spirit the things of the Spirit. ⁶For to be carnally minded is death; but to be spiritually minded is life and peace. ⁷Because the carnal mind is enmity against God: for it is not subject to the law of God, neither indeed can be. ⁸So then they that are in the flesh cannot please God. ⁹But ye are not in the flesh, but in the Spirit, if so be that

the Spirit of God dwell in you. Now if any man has not the Spirit of Christ, he is none of his. [10] And if Christ be in you, the body is dead because of sin; but the Spirit is life because of righteousness. [11] But if the Spirit of him that raised up Jesus from the dead dwell in you, he that raised up Christ from the dead shall also quicken your mortal bodies by his Spirit that dwelleth in you.

Romans 8:24-25 (KJV) [24] For we are saved by hope: but hope that is seen is not hope: for what a man seeth, why doth he yet hope for? [25] But if we hope for that we see not, then do we with patience wait for it.

Our transformed minds see the world differently and with a greater measure of compassion. The same grace that saved us was sent to operate through us in saving others. The mind of Christ we now have helps us in seeing other people just like God sees them.

Once we see from heavens unlimited vantage point and not our own conditional vision, we will recognize the countless opportunities God has provided for us to tell others about His goodness we have received,. They need to know that that grace is also available to them.

Thankfully, all of those who God sent to strengthen me and the Word of God I received in my new church gave me the power and the unction to go and serve others like never before. Now that I was no longer controlled by my fears I wanted to help others find the splendor of my King. His loving words began to replace the stony places in my heart with flesh. I started to understand that sharing the love of God requires you to have first received it.

We have to stop waiting and even declaring that others will get what they deserve and remember that no one who really comes to Christ will ever get what they truly deserve. Instead, once we have received Christ, we will get favor and the empowerment to share the message of forgiveness and love we have received. Don't let your past be a deterrent either, no matter how bad you might think it was! Our healed, rejuvenated heart and mind will serve as a witness to others of God's goodness and that witness will draw them. The same measure of faith through the Holy Ghost that empowered us to prosper and obtain every promise of God will also empower us to share the gospel by the obedience of our faith.

Favor not only opens supernatural doors to our blessings, but also has the power to open the doors to men's hearts and prepare them for the seed of God's word that we are to sow. In this way, we fulfill God's desire, "Be fruitful and increase in number; fill the earth and subdue it......"

I hope as you receive your restoration in Christ, you also accept the ability to hear the voice of Christ urging you even as he did Peter, "the devil desired to sift you, but I have prayed for you and when you are restored, go and strengthen your brother.

CHAPTER 8

THE END OF THE MATTER

When I was a child, we spent many summers with my grandmother. I recall the long road trips that included going through the Pennsylvania turnpike. Those trips seemed to take forever, but once we got to Grandma's house, the journey was well worth the drive. Her house was so peaceful that it was almost as if time stood still. The days seemed to slowly roll by with no thoughts of anything except whatever activities we found to occupy our time. I was young the last time I visited her, but I have vivid memories of the times I spent there. Those childhood memories include stretching out across my grandmother's bed on lazy summer days. Though I often fought taking my afternoon naps, I now warmly remember those times of fighting sleep as I lay on the handmade quilt thrown on her bed. I didn't want to sleep with so much to do and explore around grandma's house. There were trees to climb and fields to run through and gardens filled with strange looking vegetables that we picked and she cooked to perfection. A nap seemed like such a waste of time, but each day while watching the curtains blow back and forth in the summer breeze, I would eventually drift off to sleep. I wish I had that restful time now and think back to how wonderful it felt to not only slip into long, peaceful sleep, but slowly emerge from that sleep. I slept so soundly that it would usually take me a few minutes to fully wake up. I would lay there listening to the sound of my uncles on the front porch discussing the days catch at the nearby pond, or the familiar voices of my mom and grandmother in the kitchen. These were days that I felt completely safe and happy. The peace I experienced in that modest home in Richmond, Virginia was one I tried to replicate for years. With the exception of those mandatory afternoon naps, I don't recall having a care in the world.

Unfortunately, as the years rolled by, the challenges of life ultimately clouded out much of the hope that I had of regaining that place of peace and rest. Over time, I gave up some of that hope, replacing it with fear and bitterness.

Though it was always available to me, I did not recognize or even comprehend fully the benefit of God's comfort and shelter. My desire to be protected and experience that safety again pushed me to erect a shelter of my own. The quest for acceptance and unconditional love was fruitless without God, and instead took me right through the enemy's camp, but God can take even our dry places and squeeze out something that will nourish others. My journey, though painful for me at times, has been transformed into a purposeful one. As I emerged from the dark places where I had been a prisoner to fear and doubt, I not only understand what I did to end up there, but how to get out and I have committed to share that information with others. All of my trials served as the catalyst for my victories in Christ. I may have stayed on the road of hopelessness far too long, but I am convinced now that even the suffering was filled with divine purpose.

I can remember traveling for work before GPS systems were so available and I depended heavily on directions I followed either using a map or occasionally from something I had painstakingly printed from my computer. I once drove across the country with nothing more than a few pieces of paper with the directions from my home to my destination. For the most part, I could get there if I read the directions properly, but every now and then, I needed some help interpreting what I had read and I had to pull off the road for additional instructions.

Living the exceeding and abundant life in Christ requires much the same thing. The word of God is our direction and those He has called to teach us, especially the Holy Spirit, are our ready help if we are having trouble interpreting where we should go next. If the direction said go straight and you've turned left, please allow me to encourage you that it is never, never too late to get back on the road.

God is so awesome, He is even able to bring meaningful truths out of some of our ill-advised side roads that can help us and others stay on or get back on track. I believe this is one of the reasons I always loved reading about Paul's great adventures in the bible. If I've learned anything from looking at Paul's life, it is that the journey may not always lead down roads that one would choose to go down, but God will never make you go alone. The leading of the Holy Spirit will forever be with you to assure that you don't stray too far from the path and though there will be the occasional thorn along the way to remind you of your need for God's strength, there is no situation you will ever face that Christ hasn't already overcome.

Hebrews 13:5 reminds us that God said He will never, never leave us or forsake us. There were times, I felt absolutely alone and misunderstood, but God was there. I felt like the weight of the world was resting on my shoulders. I even felt, as I lay in that small apartment after leaving my husband like my heart had been smashed in a thousand pieces, still, God was right there with me. I didn't always recognize Him or yield myself to His voice, but it didn't stop His relentless pursuit of me until I was totally overtaken with His goodness and mercy.

Psalms 23:6 (KJV) ⁶ Surely goodness and mercy shall follow me all the days of my life: and I will dwell in the house of the LORD forever.

Don't wait to see it to believe it. Believe it, and I promise you'll see it. If you'd asked me as I lay in that darkened apartment so many years ago, I would have shouted that my heart would never mend nor trust anyone again. I would have shared that I did not have the capacity to be loved, much less love. Trusting God opens us up to believing we not only are loved, but lovable. I learned by experiencing the fullness of God that His best can include not just equipping you, but other people who have been fashioned to meet your needs. I praise God that for me, second chances also meant second (last) marriages too! Don't ever believe that life can't start

235

over, no matter how bad your past may have been. God is the God of restoration and when He puts us and our lives back together, we are better than we've ever been before. Experiencing perfect love from God provides the endless hope that is needed to embrace the joys as well as the tests that come from sharing your life with others. Once you discover the real you, the one buried in Christ, you are able to love and accept love like never before.

The greatest thing about receiving Christ and the gift of salvation is that it begins a journey with God that is never ending. We need not have regrets about the things we should have done, or could have done if only we had known what we know now. When you enter into Christ, you enter into eternity! The abundant life that is promised to all of God's children is ours not only in this world, but the one to come.

There are simply not enough words to show God how thankful I am for saving me and setting me free. *The life I now live, I live by the faith in the son of God who called me out of darkness into His marvelous light.* I have the victory by faith, the victory that makes me a world overcomer. I am no longer in darkness because His word is like a lamp to enlighten my feet so that the right path is clearly visible. I am eternally grateful for His unfailing love.

I was so afraid of failure that there are things I didn't even try. Understanding that God's mercy and grace will catch you if you fall gives you the courage to do things you've never done. The abundant life God promised begins with our belief that we are entitled to it and have been equipped with everything we need to attain it. This doesn't by any means indicate that I don't battle with doubt from time to time, but I have good weaponry! The constant communion with the Holy Spirit means that I have access to answers before I let my mind go too far beyond what I know is true. Now when I am beginning to stress over a call or bill or situation, I can hear the voice of God simply whisper, "Do you trust me?" I dare not say no! In those seasons, thank God, I remember that He is my provider and healer, and strength, always present with me, the lover of my soul, redeemer from every curse and so much more. Those truths are the assurance I need that I will never have to work again to obtain what Christ freely gave me. I realize that all the years of working did not entitle me to grace, but they did negate the grace I had been given.

My greatest hindrance to living a life that was rooted in heavenly places was me. Thankfully, once I moved me out of the way, and whole heartedly allowed my saving grace to take control, I received an all access pass to the riches of heaven here on earth and eternal life in the world to come.

I pray that you have been presented with ideas that have challenged the obstacles in your life. I would only hope that even as you have shared in part of my testimony, you've considered the resources God provided to impact yours. I am thankful for those along my journey who not only diligently knocked on the door inviting Christ into their lives, but left spiritual bread along the way so that I might also follow in Christ's footsteps. I am also eternally grateful for Christ who is the greatest expression of love the universe will ever know. I was love deprived. I don't say this because there were not folks around me that loved me; I say this because there is absolutely nothing like the love of God, especially if you are doubtful and fearful as I was. His love is perfect, so perfect that it casts out all fear. When you know our Savior and understand the motivation of God's heart as He pours out His favor on us, you will find the confidence needed to overcome life's challenges. My past was glorious, painful, humbling and the source of assurance I now have in the power of God's grace.

The seed of God's word when planted on fertile ground will bring a harvest. I pray that as we grow in the knowledge of Him we also grow in our ability to spread the good news about our Savior Jesus Christ to a world that so desperately needs truth.

God has given us some wonderful tools with which to access His power and resources and live a victorious, peaceful life, but we must utilize them. Once my heart was trained on the things of God, so were my emotions and intellect. There are still times when my faith is tested and sometimes I have to take a makeup test, but ultimately, I know what to do to fortify the battle ground of my mind and guard my heart. My constant contact with God gives me the confidence that it is His voice I hear and not my own. I study His word often and the more I know about Him, the more I understand His will for me versus my own fleshly desires.

I finally realized that the word of God was not some harsh threat of God's punishment for my wrongs. The kind of love God has for you can't be received by fear. Remember that while the Bible outlines in detail the wages for rejecting Christ and remaining in a life of sin, God's word is not a threat. It is a prophecy that is presented to us to reveal the person of Christ and the power of God's love.

When I heard the voice of Jesus sharing truths with me instead of the voice of an angry God giving me a stern warning, my life changed. The more you understand the workings of God through Christ, the more you understand that you can trust and put your confidence in Him. That means that in a world where it is difficult to separate those who are for you from those who are against you, you can always count on Him.

There is indescribable peace in knowing that God is someone we can trust and depend on, who will never leave us. Our creator is with us at all times and has more than demonstrated His love for us and His desire to love us eternally. Finally, after all of the roads, and side roads, and wrong roads, and all of the paths, and alleys I traveled, I've found the source of every good thing. I am complete in Christ.

It is hard to top those wonderful days of drifting into peaceful sleep as I lay on my grandma's bed tracing the images of her quilts with my little fingers. But nothing can compare to the peace, joy, contentment and wholeness that comes from receiving the love of a father who daily demonstrates His love for us. Never doubt His willingness to give you His best. He already did. If you can change your mind, even if you have tried before, you can change your life. He is after all the God of another second chance.

My Prayer for You

Lord, I thank you that the individuals who have read this book have received the incorruptible seed of your word. I thank you that it will be planted on the good ground of their hearts creating some thirty, sixty and a hundred fold. I declare that your word is pregnant with faith that opens the doors to endless possibilities and they will see your goodness in the land of the living.   I praise you that your Spirit, even the Holy Spirit, the Spirit of Truth is leading them and guiding them today into all truth. Lord I declare that this spirit testifies together with their spirit that they are your children and therefore heirs and joint heirs with Christ. As joint heirs, they have an entitlement to everything in heaven and the dominating power to establish the things that are in heaven on the earth.   Where they are weak today Lord I ask for your strength acknowledging that it is not by power or might, but by your Spirit that things are possible through us. I ask that you would encourage them for we know that while weeping may endure for a night, joy is sure to come in the morning. You promised that those who share Christ's suffering will also share His authority to reign. Lord I acknowledge that it is the Spirit that gives life and the flesh profits them nothing therefore I rejoice that they receive the words that you speak for they are spirit and they are life. I thank you that whosoever is born of God is victorious over the world; and this is the victory that conquers the world, even our faith.

Now Father I am eternally grateful that your word will not return to you void, but has accomplished everything you desired. It has uprooted old thoughts and planted your concepts and precepts that lead to abundant life. I praise you that they will meditate in your word day and night and will continue to cultivate a relationship with you so that they can easily identify your voice and a stranger's voice they will not hear and follow, but only the voice of their shepherd. I honor you for abundant peace, even the peace that surpasses all understanding in their lives and finally declare that what you've placed in them, even the power to draw the world, will be contagious and will bring forth much fruit. Now Father I thank you that their lives will never be the same, but will only grow more fertile and they will receive with gladness your love and forever share that love as they praise your holy and righteous name, in Jesus Name, amen.